A SIGN OF THINGS TO COME

More Dialogues with St. Padre Pio

Volume 2

Orest Stocco

A Sign of Things to Come

ISBN 978-1-926-442-20-4

Edited by Penny Lynn Cates
Cover Design by Penny Lynn Cates

A Note from the Author

My dialogues with St. Padre Pio are a mystery to me. I do not know whether it is the Roman Catholic Saint who suffered the wounds of Jesus most of his life that I am conversing with, or a figment of my imagination, my creative unconscious, my muse, or my higher self; all I know is that my dialogues with St. Padre Pio are good for me. They help resolve my issues.

Journal writing could do this also, and so could a daily diary; but not as well. Something magical happens when I engage St. Padre Pio, something that I cannot put my finger on but which I know helps to heal my wounded soul, and that's all that really matters to me.

"Life is a journey of the self," St. Padre Pio said to me when he was channeled by a gifted psychic medium for my novel *Healing with Padre Pio,* which became my inspiration for these dialogues (prompted by Carl Jung's technique of active imagination); but every soul's journey through life is different, and it's this difference that fascinates readers.

This is the appeal of literature, whatever the genre may be; and, with a little luck, my dialogues with St. Padre Pio will draw you into my story, if only for a little while. Hopefully, it will be a happy, rewarding reading experience.

Orest Stocco,
Georgian Bay, Ontario
November 1, 2018

Dialogues

1. Let's Talk 1

2. Earth to Padre 4

3. New England Clam Chowder.....................7

4. The American Election............................10

5. Looking for Some Advice 13

6. What`s Life For? 15

7. On the Writer Philip Roth 17

8. Getting Bored with Writers 20

9. Our First Snowfall 23

10. So, It's Time for the Sequel? 26

11. New Year: 2017....................................29

12. My Hemingway Notebook 32

13. Author Tom Harpur Dies 35

14. Down with a Cold.................................37

15. Keeping a Journal, of a Sort 39

16. The Labyrinth of the Mind 43

17. Feeling Overwhelmed Again.................47

18. River of Karma.....................................50

19. The Mote in the Eye 53

20. Want to Run Away... 56

21. Not a Funk, but Something...58

22. Here We Go Again 61

23. Another Book Brought Home 62

24. Talk Time 65

25. What Now Brown Cow? 66

26. "You're a Fraud!"...70

27. I Feel Like I'm Out at Sea, Floundering 72

28. What's Wrong with this Picture?................................75

29. You Did Promise to Keep Me Safe 78

30. Deep Talk, Please? 81

31. Interrupted Chat...84

32. A Spiritual Musing For My Russian Readers 87

33. Not Feeling Creative 90

34. A Sexual Metaphor for British Imperialism................93

35. Losing My Fire 96

36. The Way of Passion...99

37. On the Discovery of a New Poet 102

38. On the Philosophy of No-self...................................106

39. She Wants More Padre 109

40. Alone, but Never Lonely 111

41. Like a Fly Flitting on Water 115

42. A Thanksgiving Story 117

43. Oh No, a Directive from My Muse! 120

44. Don`t Know What to Say 122

45. My Demon Fears 125

46. Cards on the Table...127

47. There's No End to Anxiety 130

48. Can't I Go One Week Without Anxiety?....................132

49. Christmas Day: 2017 134

50. New Year's Day: 2018..136

51. My Amazon Wish List Christmas Gift.....................138

52. The Thin Edge of the Wedge...............................141

53. An Idea for a New Book.....................................145

54. A Big Thank You 148

55. The Deal's Almost Closed 150

56. The Deal Has Closed...155

57. Looking for Focus 157

58. Second Dentist Appointment...............................159

59. The Extraction 163

60. My Dental Appointment Went Well 167

61. Extracting My Phobia..170

62. Extraction Postponed..172

63. Shadow Pushback..174

64. Today I'm (!) Old..177

65. Going up North...180

66. The Humbling Begins 182

67. Back from Our Getaway................................184

68. A Consolidating Experience.........................188

69. Can We Talk, Please?...................................192

70. Terrifying Dream Last Night........................196

71. Lost Again in a Strange City 199

72. From Order to Chaos....................................201

73. Please Bring Her Back to Me Safe and Whole..........204

74. Where do I Start?...206

75. Not Quite There Yet... 208

1. Let's Talk

"Good morning, Padre. The last time we talked was August 30, a little over a month ago, but it feels like much longer, and I miss our dialogues; so, if you don't mind, I'm going to open another file and ask if you'd like to join me in another discourse. It's just a way of keeping in touch with my creative unconscious. Are you up to the initiative?"

"I've been waiting patiently for you to connect again. You need an outlet for your feelings; and yes, another file of discourses would be the perfect solution. It will get you motivated again so you can begin a new book. I'm very pleased with your twin soul books (Death, the Final Frontier, and The Merciful Law of Divine Synchronicity). They turned out much better than I expected, if you can believe that."

"Yes, I can believe it because I am free to let my creative unconscious flow of its own will, and where it goes no-one knows, not even you—until, that is, you tune in to that specific frequency. Correct?"

"Correct. To know the future, one has to tune into the frequency one wishes to know about, which isn't something we should talk about today. Let's just concentrate on what's on your mind for now, shall we?"

"Let me get a cup of coffee first. Give me a moment, please."

"By all means..."

"Okay, I've got my coffee and am free to talk. I don't know where to begin; perhaps a word or two about my twin soul books just to get this new discourse started. I'm ready to hand them over to Penny for editing and formatting. She downloaded her Wizard program again, but had to pay for it because she lost her program this summer when her computer crashed and she lost all her files; but she's ready to take on my new books and get them published on Lulu. I can't wait to see the covers for these books. We're going to get

Death, the Final Frontier out first, and a few months down the road we'll put out *The Merciful Law of Divine Synchronicity*; but I'm stalling, Padre. I know we ended our last discourse with you encouraging me to get into short story writing, and I even tried this morning by opening up my file on the stories I've written so far; but I wasn't in the mood. That's when I decided to reconnect with you. What's going on with me, anyway?"

*"Well, you have spent yourself on your twin soul books, plus all of the poetry that you are writing. After all, you did write one complete book of poetry also this summer (*Not My Circus, Not My Monkeys*), so you have been writing and expending yourself; now you are in the process of filling up the well, as the saying goes. Just let your creative well replenish itself and then you can continue with your short story writing. It will happen soon enough."*

"That's why I had to reconnect with you. You're so encouraging! I was drying up, and I was feeling very flat; especially yesterday. It was a strange day. I felt like I was myself but not myself, like I was on a vacation away from myself. It was a strange feeling. I felt like my 'I' was free of itself but without a sense of a loss of my identity, a very strange sensation. What was that all about, anyway?"

"This is the sensation of the selfless self. You passed through the eye of the needle and are free to grow in your selfless self, and yesterday you had a very strong impression of your selfless self because of the twin soul books that you have just written. The spiritual benefit that you have earned by writing those books is beginning to show itself in the growth of your selfless self. You had a growth spurt yesterday, and you felt it. Your selfless self is the fruit of your life-tree, and you are going to experience a lot more of your selfless self until you realize that this is the new self that you gave birth to in your journey of self-discovery. It will be a wonderful place to be, I assure you. Just let it happen."

"I may have a poem in this feeling!"

"Indeed, you may. Your poetry is exciting your readers on social media. They don't quite know what to make of it. You force them to think, and some are afraid of your poetry because it forces them to think. But keep posting. They look forward to it regardless how it makes them feel. It's good for them. It wakes them up."

2

A Sign of Things to Come

"What do you think of the idea of posting a short story next Saturday. I was thinking of my story "Artsy Lady." I'd like to introduce my readers to my short stories."

"Not just yet. Post your poetry for another month or two before you start posting your short stories. Give them a good taste of your poetry first."

"I have to do some morning chores before Penny goes to work—make our Essiac tea and smoothie, take out the garbage, and other little chores—so I'll get back to you later, if you don't mind the interruptions."

"Not at all. Do your chores and we'll chat another day."

"Thank you, Padre."

"You're welcome, my friend...

2. Earth to Padre

"Earth to Padre...come in, please. I'm in danger of falling into a funk and need some guidance; or, if not guidance, some propping up. I'm not going to beat around the bush: I'm disappointed in how my poetry is being received on social media, and this is discouraging. I thought poetry would be a better medium to get my point across, whatever the point might be that my poems wish to make; but very little response discourages me. I'm thinking of going silent for a while and concentrate on my book of short stories. What do you think?"

"Yes, the response to your poetry is not as you would like it to be; but poetry is not for everyone. Those that read your poems are intrigued by your point of view, and it does make them think; but thinking is not something people like to do these days. Go ahead and take some time off. Don't post any poems for two or three months and see what happens when you do post again, just to see if you were missed or not. Concentrate on your stories."

"I'm having trouble consolidating my energies. I feel almost spent. I felt so low in energy the other day that it felt like the wick of my fire had almost gone out, and I could feel it wanting to burn out completely; and you know what, Padre? I wanted it to go out!"

"That's not an uncommon feeling for one whose fire has burned so white. You have done what you came to do, and you are eager to return; but you cannot, because your love for Penny is much too strong. You will see your life through, and it will be complete. Do not concern yourself with the fire of your life. It will always burn bright."

"Now we come to the real issue of this talk: my feeling out of place in this world. I honestly cannot make heads or tails of it. The world is so far at odds with how I am and feel that I honestly get the feeling I'm living in a parallel world."

"You do so much remind me of my own life. How often I felt like I did not belong in the world I was living in. The world came to

me in my confessional, and I lived the life of every penitent that came to me; but so removed was I from their world that I did not know how to reconcile my feelings with my penitents. It was always a trial for me. Here's what I did to adjust to the world: I prayed to God for guidance. I prayed, and prayed, and prayed the rosary every moment of the day. I prayed in my mind everywhere I went. You need a focal point for your energies. You need to find a center of gravity that will collect your energies like prayer collected mine. Your writing should be your focal point."

"And don't worry about the world?"

"Yes. Let the world be. Concentrate on your writing, your stories. Get them written and perfect your craft of story writing. It will grow exponentially with the time you put into it, I promise you. And you will be amazed at how good you will become at story writing."

"Penny wants me to concentrate on story writing. She's tired of my other writing. She's very, very tired of it. And you know what? So am I! But I had to do it, Padre. I had to do that kind of writing to get to where I had to be to resolve all the issues of my life."

"Not many people can boast such accomplishment. You followed your nudges, and they took you to where you had to be to resolve your issues; and now you are free of them. This gives you the luxury of anxiety-free creativity, which is the best type of energy to write with because it allows the energy to find its own way without interruptions. You will learn this as you proceed with your story writing. Give it a chance and see what happens."

"Well, I do have four stories already typed in for my book of stories *Sparkles in the Mist*, and I've started on my fifth story "The Amethyst Broach," so I do feel like I'm getting somewhere. They do need tightening up and some editing, but on the whole I'm very pleased with them. What do you think of them?"

"You know that I cannot wait for you to devote yourself to story writing, because story writing is where all your writing skills come together; and to answer your question, I am more than pleased with what you have done so far. As you said, they do need some work; but not as much as to disrupt the spontaneity of the stories. That's their genius."

"I'm thinking of going from this book of stories straight to my novel *An Atheist, An Agnostic, and Me* because they involve the same

5

characters and I will have a much deeper feeling about them when I complete *Sparkles in the Mist*. What do you think?"

"That novel needs to be out there. That's all I have to say."

"You're not shutting down on me, are you?"

"No, I cannot shut down on you. All I am saying is that you really have no choice but to complete that novel, because it is a very big part of your life; and your life being so unique, this novel has to be out there for your readers to see what it means to live the life of a seeker who never stops seeking until he finds what he's looking for. That novel will be an inspiration for many, many, many—and I mean MANY readers!"

"I feel better already. Thank you, Padre."

"You're welcome...."

3. New England Clam Chowder

"Good morning, Padre. I thought I'd start my day with a little chat because yesterday's chat got me inspired and it turned out to be a good day. I began typing my story "The Amethyst Broach" into my file, then had breakfast which Penny made, French Toast, and then we did some leaf blowing in our front yard. We've already blown leaves three or four times already, but we can't wait for them all to fall off the trees so we do them incrementally just to stay on top of them. Penny took a break and went into the house to put on some New England Clam Chowder, and when we did our leaf blowing, we sat on our front deck visiting with our neighbors—Rosanne and her little boy, who's about a year and a half, and our retired neighbor. Her husband didn't come over, which was a surprise because he always drops over just for the company. He's a lonely man I might add, but that's another story for another time. Anyway, after our visit we went in for dinner, and I put on a nice fire in our air-tight Pacific Western wood stove and Penny put on some cheese biscuits for our chowder, and we had a beautiful dinner. So, it turned out to be a very nice day, Padre; and I'm glad we had our little chat because it got my day started."

"You're welcome, my friend. Every day can be this way as long as you maintain the right attitude. It's all a question of frequency, as you know; and establishing the right frequency is what the new teaching is all about. But as you say, it's the same old wine put into a new bottle. Right attitude would be better. Why don't we talk about that for now?"

"Sure. But I'm going to get a cup of coffee first, if you don't mind."

"Not at all…"

"Okay, I got my coffee and turned the air down on the fire so it can burn slowly. I found it this morning almost burned out, but there were enough coals to reignite the fire so I added a couple of pieces of nice dry hardwood that we got delivered to our house last Friday and which I piled into our garage for our winter burning, and now the fire is burning fine. We love wood heating, Padre; it changes the whole atmosphere of the house. I might even go so far as to say that it energizes us somehow. Is there any truth to this?"

"Plenty of truth. The atmosphere of a house affects the mood of its inhabitants, and if you have a nice cozy fire in the fireplace, or air tight wood stove with a glass door that allows you to see the flames burning, as you have,) it creates a nice, warm, cozy atmosphere which is conducive to feelings of warmth. Yes, it does certainly energize you. This is a good introduction to the right attitude that we should talk about today."

"Off the top of my head, I would say that the right attitude is graced with the virtue of giving. Let me illustrate what I mean by this. While Penny was making cheese biscuits for her New England Clam Chowder that she wanted to make today for our fall leafing, I said to her: "Your nice dinner deserves a nice fire." So, I put on a fire; and by the time the biscuits came out of the oven the fire was burning brightly and the atmosphere of our sun room and kitchen was changed and made our dinner very enjoyable. And after dinner Penny had a short rest on the living room couch while I watched the news on the American election on TV, and then I took Penny out for coffee and a long drive so we could catch the waning fall colors. That's how our day went. But the point I want to make is that Penny thanked me for putting on a nice fire for our New England Clam Chowder, and for taking her out for coffee and a nice long drive to catch the colors before the leaves fall and winter sets in. And then we're into a whole new season."

"So, what you're saying is that your little gestures of lighting a fire to make your house nice and cozy to add to your enjoyment of dinner and then taking Penny out for coffee and nice drive were gestures of love that go into making up the attitude that one needs to have a good day, and a good life?"

"I guess that's what I'm saying. Which means that this attitude that we want to unravel is essentially about love. By cultivating and PRACTICING love—and by this, I mean putting love into action, not simply thinking about it —creates the higher frequency that one needs to have a good day every day; right?"

A Sign of Things to Come

"Absolutely! It's all about giving at the right time. Timing is very important in the creation of this attitude that determines the frequency for a good day and good life. One must give of oneself at the right moment, otherwise the gesture loses its meaning."

"I agree. Timing is vital to the process. What good does it do after the fact? It's all a question of aligning the variables of one's life so they are in sync with the love that is at the center of life—hey, have I got something here?"

"You do. Love is the core mystery of life. Love is life, but tapping into love is what the mystery is all about; and yesterday you tapped into love with your gestures of lighting a fire for you and your love to enjoy the special dinner that Penny made for you, along with the cheese biscuits, and then taking her out for coffee and a nice long drive. It was a nice way to cap your day. Love is at the heart of this attitude that we're unraveling. Now I think you can get on with your story. So, have a nice day, my friend; and until we talk again."

"Okay. Thank you for this. It's a great way to start my day…"

4. The American Election

November 4, 2016

"Good morning, Padre. I'd like to start the day with a conversation with you, I don't know what about yet, but I just need to get motivated and I know that talking with you gets me primed with inspiration. Let me begin by saying that yesterday I did some leaf blowing and reading some short stories from a book called *Wonderful Town, New York Stories from The New Yorker*, edited by David Remnick, and I think I've got the feeling for what a New Yorker story is all about; but I have to share something with you, if I may?"

"By all means."

"Reading those New Yorker stories boosts my confidence in my own story writing, because the book of stories that I'm working on now are no less engaging, and even more so than the stories I've read so far in *Wonderful Town*. I hope I'm not being overconfident, but I don't think so. I haven't finished typing in my story "The Amethyst Broach yet, but I hope to do so today. So, am I overconfident?"

"I would not say so. Your stories have a literary quality all of their own, not to be compared with the New Yorker stories. They could be read as a New Yorker story, but they go beyond the limited literary confines of the New Yorker stories because of the subject matter. You take the reader to new places that no writer for the New Yorker can take them. This makes your stories better, because it opens up the reader to new dimensions of reality that the New Yorker refuses to explore. Just keep on doing what you are doing. Your stories will catch on once you get them out there. So far, I like the stories you've typed in and can't wait for the rest."

"Okay, Padre; on to some serious stuff, if I may—the American election. I'm not so sure Hillary Clinton is going to win anymore. Donald Trump is gaining ground, and I don't know whether to laugh or cry. But as I said to Penny the other day, America gets what America deserves. Does America deserve a man as crude as Donald Trump? What's going on there, anyway?"

"The American psyche is being exposed for what it has become, and Donald Trump has become the symbol of the American shadow. You are correct to say that he's the dark side of the American personality, and if he wins the election it's because America has to see itself for what it has become. Donald Trump is holding up a mirror for the American people to see their dark side."

"But if he's elected, what will that do to global politics?"

"Shake it up."

"Will that be a good thing, though?"

"The world is in the middle of a transformation from complacency to clarity, and it needs a good shakeup to get there. Donald Trump serves life too, and his service will be to facilitate this transformation. Whether he wins or not depends upon how much the American people want change."

"Would it be fair to say that the American election boils down to CHANGE or MORE OF THE SAME? Or is that too simple?"

"Essentially, that is what it comes down to; but it does involve the need to clean house, which can never be done because the house is the system, and the system is what politics is all about. You cannot change the system. The system will always regenerate itself according to the people. The only way to change the system is to change the individual, and the individual needs to see that he is a reflection of the system; but who wants to see themselves in that light? That's the dilemma of the American election. The people do not want to acknowledge their own shadow."

"It doesn't really matter who gets in, then?"

"It does matter, because the person who gets in brings with them their own baggage; and this can determine the new direction of the country. All I am saying is that the direction will always be the system, because the system is the people."

"This is a conundrum, isn't it? To change the world, the individual has to change; and for the individual to change, he/she has to transform their shadow, is that it? People have to change their attitude about life?"

"They have to change their expectations. As long as man continues to believe that this life is all about the self and not the other,

then life will continue to create the system that controls the people. It is a conundrum."

"You know what, Padre; that's the feeling I got from all the stories that I read so far in *Wonderful Town*—a feeling that the people in these stories were trapped in cycles of becoming, a never-ending process with no way out. Somerset Maugham, a master craftsman of the short story, implies what I'm trying to say in his comment about the *New Yorker* story. He defined them as, "those wonderful *New Yorker* stories which always end up when the hero goes away, but he doesn't really go away, does he?" Implying, as I said, the circularity of life—hence, the conundrum!"

"Exactly. That's why your stories are different. They are aware of the conundrum, and they offer a way out. This should be your motivation for writing your stories. You can't possibly find greater inspiration than this."

"Thank you for this. I'll finish typing in "The Amethyst Broach" today and begin my next story. Until we talk again…"

5. Looking for Some Advice

Sunday, November 6, 2016

"Good morning, Padre. I'd like some advice. Nothing major, just a question about how to capture my reader's interest. I posted my short story "The Genius of Updike" on my spiritual musings blog yesterday, but I didn't generate the interest that I thought my story would get, and I'd like to ask you what I can do to pull the readers in. I thought of introducing my fictional self character and give the story some context to entice the reader. What do you think?"

"That would be a good enticement, but you must make your character interesting enough so the reader will find in him what they are missing in their own life. This is why readers read stories. They are looking for what they don't have and would like to have. What does your narrator self have that the reader would want?"

"He has found an answer to life's purpose and meaning and he is living it. This is a terribly presumptuous thing to say, because one is not supposed to know this answer. It's okay to be a seeker, but it's not okay to find what you are seeking; because once you find it you set yourself apart from the rest of the world, and the world will resent you for it. That's Oriano's dilemma."

"Then you must word it so it will catch your reader's interest. Oriano has a secret that he cannot share with the world, but he knows that the world wants it but cannot accept it when it gets it; that's Oriano's dilemma. How does he say what he feels compelled to say as a writer?"

"I'm going to write a precis of my story. Please guide my thoughts…"

Introducing the first story of my new book of short stories *Sparkles in the Mist.* "The Genius of Updike" is a story about an aspiring writer's dilemma. Oriano, the narrator of the story, wanted to become a writer since high school; but he had to suspend his calling to pursue a higher calling that took many years to satisfy. Now he's back and wants to reconnect with his calling to write stories like his literary mentor Ernest Hemingway, but he feels it may be too late. "The Genius of Updike" is Oriano's re-entry into creative writing, a dynamic that is played out with his friends Leo Kubochev and Boris Petrochenko. The conflict of the story lies in their separate philosophies: Leo is an agnostic, Boris an atheist, and Oriano a believer who defies description. But what is it that Oriano believes that both intrigues and frustrates his friends, and everyone who meets him? This is the mystery of "The Genius of Updike," and the stories to follow…

"Okay, Padre; that's my precis. What do you think?"
"That should do it. Post it along with the link to your blog and see what happens."
"I'll do that after I have Penny read it. Thank you."
"You're welcome…"

6. What`s Life For?

"Good morning, Padre. The madness of the American election is over, and it looks like the American people wanted a shake-up in their political system; they voted Donald Trump for their president, and now the fun begins. Trump gave voice to the 'forgotten people', and now we will see how much Trump cares for them. The next four years should be interesting. But I want to ask you a question. I'm hesitant to post five new poems today on my blog. What do you think I should do? I just feel some doubt about posting, and don't really know why."

"You fear rejection. But that should not stop you. Post your five new poems and let your reader get a glimpse on the world from the perspective of an awakened soul. Don't be afraid to put your poetry out there. It speaks a new language. Trust your gift, my friend."

"I finished typing in another story the other day, "The Frenchman's Notebook." I like this story. I have six stories typed in now, and four more to go to complete my book *Sparkles in the Mist*. And yesterday I watched some videos on John Updike. He inspires me, and I want to read some of his stories as I work on mine. I think he's a wonderful writer, and reading him helps me polish my own stories. I didn't get as much response as I expected for my story "The Genius of Updike," but that's okay. It takes time, I know; but it does get frustrating waiting."

"Your books will find their place in the world. Do what you are called to do, and let God take care of the rest."

"I think that in the end it all comes down to just doing what we feel we should do, doesn't it? After all, you did say that life is a journey of the self. So, what does it matter what the world thinks, as long as we fulfill our destined purpose. Right?"

"Essentially, yes; but we do not live in a vacuum. We are all connected by our humanity, and we must contribute to the process, or what's life for?"

"I don't feel the inspiration this morning. I'm going to go and get my weekend papers later and spend my day reading them, and maybe do some more leafing. Most of the leaves have fallen off our trees now, but I have five or six piles to dispose of. I'm still in a quandary as to post my poems or not. I think I'll just let this ride for the day. Maybe tomorrow. I'll see. Sorry, Padre; but I just don't have it in me to continue. Until the next time."

"Take the day and let it unfold accordingly. I'll be here when you need me."

"Thank you. *Ciao* for now, then…"

7. On the Writer Philip Roth

Thursday, November 17, 2016

"Good morning, Padre. I've been watching some You Tube videos on the writer Philip Roth, and as much as I was averse to his personal energy, I confess that I enjoyed his life story; meaning, how he used his own life for his fiction. An internationally famous writer who is studied at university, it was fascinating watching how professors and reader understood him; but the best explanation for his fiction was his own fiction, because in his fiction he tells his life story. That's the genius of his fiction and the reason for his popularity. He presents the human condition as he experienced it, but he does so through the magnifying lens of his imagination, and the rest is mystery. There's no resolution to his fiction, only more of the human condition; and because he believes that we have no central self, the human condition is nothing but a process of living with no inherent purpose. And readers like this for some inexplicable reason. Or does Philip Roth simply confirm their misery?"

"Every life is a struggle, and Philip Roth writes about his life in the struggle. Readers can relate to this. But as you say, he offers no solution to the struggle and simply dives into it deeper and deeper and deeper. And the deeper he dives into the struggle, the more dark and mysterious his books become; but still, he offers no resolution. This is why you were never attracted to his writing. Intuitively, you knew he had nothing for you. But now that you have found your way out of the struggle, you are interested in his life and writing for literary purposes; and, if you give him a chance, he has much to teach you."

"That's the feeling I got watching all those interviews online. He has given me permission to write about my own life with much more literary freedom. And I may just try a story or two in his style just to see where they will go. Something strangely comic, or ironic; I don't know."

"It would be liberating. Give it some thought."

"I've only read one of Roth's novels, *Portnoy's Complaint*, and one short story, "Smart Money," but from these two stories I get the feel of his autobiographical fiction; and watching half a dozen interviews of him discussing his novels has given me permission to experiment more with my own fiction, and I may just venture one day to write a story that stretches the material of my life like Roth stretched his. What do you say, Padre?"

"The imagination is infinitely stretchable, and you can let it use your material at its will; but this requires much courage. That was Roth's victory. And defeat."

"Why defeat? Because it took him too deep into the darkness of the human condition and he couldn't get himself out? Could he not redeem himself through his fiction?"

"No. That's what makes him a tragic writer."

"Why do readers love to read about the dark? The poet/singer Leonard Cohen just died and people from all over the world are paying tribute to him, but his last album that he toured the world with was called "You Wanted It Darker." Cohen sang with an ecstatic darkness. Was that the attraction? The ecstasy that he found in the darkness? That reminds me of a phrase that was used by someone in the audience responding to a Shadow Master's talk (the spiritual leader of an off-shoot Christian solar cult teaching that I studied for three years), referring to his teaching as 'the ecstasy of darkness.' That phrase scared the hell out of me when I first heard it. Now I'm almost amused by it, because there seems to be some kind of perverse joy in darkness that people like Leonard Cohen and his fans are attracted to. What's this all about, anyway?"

"You're onto something very deep here. You could say that misery loves company. This is the attraction. Misery confirms one's life, and Roth and Cohen are two different kinds of artists who confirm man's misery in their own fashion; but misery it is, nonetheless. Leonard Cohen celebrates it in his songs and poem, and Philip Roth in his fiction."

"I guess I'll never be a popular writer, then. 1 celebrate redemption from misery in my writing. That's not too appealing to the reader, because it implies accountability; and we all know that accountability is less popular than entitlement."

"Perhaps you can extend this irony in a story, or a novel?"

18

A Sign of Things to Come

"Maybe I will. Let me think on it…"

8. Getting Bored with Writers

Sunday, November 27, 2016

"Good morning, Padre. Right off the bat, let me tell you that I miss writing my spiritual musings. I know I said I wasn't going to write anymore, but I do miss writing them. They tapped me into my creative unconscious in a way that my other writing does not. and I miss that direct link-up; and you know what? I may just sit down and write a spiritual musing now and then just to tap into those spiritual musing energies. I do miss them, Padre."

"I know. When you wrote your spiritual musings, you connected with the stream of life in a way that your poetry and prose cannot connect you. Would you like to know why?"

"Please, tell me."

"Like an electric short in the wiring, your spiritual musings addressed the short in the flow of life's energy, that's why. When you wrote a spiritual musing, you gave your reader an insight into the short in their own wiring, and if they took your insights to heart they could address their short and have the life-force flow freely and effectively. So, you see, your spiritual musings did more for your reader than you realized. But as you said, sometimes your musings were too much for them. But in good time you will get back into them, just for the sake of writing them."

"I probably will. But I have a lot of other books to finish up first. I've just finished typing my short story "The Snake Man" for *Sparkles in the Mist*, and it turned out to be much better than I expected. In fact, I was even thinking of not including it in this book because I didn't think it was good enough; but I changed my mind after I worked on it. And I just started typing into my file a story called "The Death of Jacob Wentzle," but I feel about this one as I felt about "The Snake Man" (my original title for this story was "The Cusp,"), and I hope I end up liking it enough to include it in my book also. But I can't be sure until I type it all in and work on it. I'll just have to wait and see. But it would be a good transition to my story "Kimberly's Gift." What do you think?"

"I think you should give it a chance. It may be better than you think. It is a very personal story, revealing how you felt at the time; and since these stories are about your private life, I would think this story would be essential. Work on it."

"I will. Now, I have to reveal something to you. I've been watching YouTube videos of other writers. One writer in particular interested me, because of her interest in the Danish philosopher Soren Kierkegaard. Her name is Siri Hustvedt. An American Norwegian whose interest in psychiatry and psychoanalysis interested me. I watched half a dozen videos on her and then I began to notice something that bothered me, but this didn't manifest until I watched three or four videos on the American writer Richard Ford; that's when I realized that what these writers had to say bored me. Yes, they bored me. Why? Because their paradigm was too small, too constricted, to limited to the life that they lived. It just came to me that the multidimensionality of life was missing in their worldview, and this stuck out for me like a sore thumb once I noticed it. It's like they were missing the whole point of life and were dancing to the same old tired tune. I just shook my head and stopped watching. I hope their books aren't boring, which I doubt because good writers make life interesting to read. So, what do I do now for inspiration?"

"Do more reading. Read all the short stories you can to saturate yourself with the genre. It will profit you immensely for your own short story writing. Don't try to analyze the stories as you read them, just enjoy them. They will sink in deep and you will learn what you need to learn automatically. Trust your writer's instincts to pick up the lessons you need to improve your own stories. Read, read, and read some more; and watch less television. Get into the habit of reading in front of the fire. There is magic in reading in front of a wood fire. Trust me."

"Well, we have enough wood for the winter, so I'll give it a shot. What I'd love to do is go through two or three Updike books of short stories, one or two of Alice Munro's, and perhaps one or two novels by Vladimir Nabokov who is praised by everyone. I should find out for myself what all the fuss is about. I have three or four of his novels. And perhaps more Chekov. I don't know, I'll just let my writer's instinct guide me."

"Do that."

"Okay, Padre; until we chat again…"

9. Our First Snowfall

Monday, December 5, 2016

"Good morning, Padre. I just came in from shoveling the driveway. We had our first winter snowfall last night, about seven centimeters, and I hand shoveled our driveway just for the exercise. Penny wanted me to use our snow blower, but I took my time and did a little workout. It worries Penny when I do that, but I said to her, 'I have ten more books to write before I go, so don't worry about me.' (I have a damaged heart from two heart attacks, and I had open heart surgery.) And you know what, Padre; I kind of believe it. I say this, because I DO believe that our life is choreographed, and we die when we are meant to die; so, I have no choice given this belief but to play it all by ear. What do you say to that?"

"I say you have a lot of faith in God. That's a good thing. Just keep on believing that you are not going to die until you write your ten new books—which, I take to mean excludes the books that you have already written but have yet to publish?"

"Yes."

"Then just keep doing what you are doing."

"Today is one of those days where I don't feel very creative. It feels like an off day, and I just want to get through it the best I can. This is why I decided to chat with you. I know that by unloading my anxiety on you, you have a way of lifting my spirits; so, I hope you don't mind me using you this way."

"This is what I'm here for. Unload your deepest fears and anxieties and see what it does for you. Begin with your fear of not being your best in your stories. You seem to be bothered by how your Updike story reads?"

"Yes. It seems to be a bit much compared to my second story, "Just Another Day in the City." This story reads much better than my Updike story, and I feel at odds with myself."

"You have no need to be. Your Updike story has its purpose just as all of your stories have their purpose, and it's not fair to the

stories to compare them with each other. They may grow out of each other, but they all have their own purpose. This is the mystery of the creative process. So, don't fret over this. Just finish your book of stories and get it out there."

"I also got my musings together for my fourth volume of spiritual musings, *The Armchair Guru,* and I feel a little leery about it now. But I will get it out, despite my feelings because these spiritual musings address certain thoughts and feelings that I had when writing them, and I want them on record because they chart my progress through life. What do you think?"

"Exactly. They reflect your inner growth and they are a necessary addition to your body of work, your life-tree. Your spiritual musings are a record of your spiritual growth, and one day they will be appreciated for the wisdom that you have brought to your musings."

"I've been doing some online research on the writer William Styron, the author of the iconic novel *Sophie's Choice,* and I just finished watching a YouTube video of his daughter Alexandra talking about her memoir *Reading My Father,* and I had no idea that her father suffered as much as he did from chronic depression. Have I got this thing about depression all wrong?"

"Not entirely. It's a little more complicated than you make it out to be, but essentially you caught the devil by the tail, if I may borrow one of your expressions; so don't undermine yourself. You have good insights into depression, and your spiritual musings on depression give your reader much to think about."

"I'm going to read, or try to read again Styron's book *A Tidewater Morning,* a collection of three stories which I found very engaging the first time I read them. I don't have any of his novels, but I may get *Sophie's Choice* and his memoir *Darkness Visible,* the record of his decent into depression. I want to get it from the horse's mouth what depressions is all about."

"You will get a good insight into clinical depression, but this book, in spite of all of its merits, won't add or subtract from your intuitive understanding of depression; so, read it if you must, but it's not an essential requirement."

A Sign of Things to Come

"I'm back to where you always bring me, aren't I? Back to my own writing? Just write my own stories and let life reveal itself as I have experienced it; is that it?"

"Yes."

"Okay, Padre. On that note, we can call it a day. Thank you for listening."

"You're welcome, my friend..."

10. So, It's Time for the Sequel?

Friday, December 16, 2016

"I didn't expect it, Padre; but last Saturday morning while I was editing one of my stories for *Sparkles in the Mist*, Penny came into my den and asked me if I wanted to go to Orillia, and I said yes. She had seen a post on Facebook from her old boss and friend, who was celebrating the first-year anniversary of his liver transplant, and she wanted to visit him where his wife had a booth for her crafts at the Orillia Fairground Farmers' Market. I said yes, because I knew intuitively that you had nudged Penny to ask me; but I'm going not to ask you right now if you did or not, because I want to leave that until later in our chat. I just want to say right off the bat that I felt the nudge to go immediately, because I knew that the time was right for us to get together again to write a sequel to my novel *Healing with Padre Pio* that I wrote when Angie, Penny's former boss's wife, channeled you for my novel. It's been almost five years since I wrote *Healing with Padre Pio*, and I felt it was time for the sequel; and wouldn't you know, Angie also felt it because she woke up Saturday morning with me on her mind. 'I knew I would be seeing you soon,' she said when we met at her booth at the market, and that confirmed it. So, Padre; what do you say? Am I ready to write the sequel? Or, should I say, are Angie and I ready?"

"Yes, you are both ready; but it won't happen for a while yet. You have to get this book of stories finished first, and your novel. By then you will be ready for the sequel to Healing with Padre Pio. *But this sequel may surprise you, because it might not be written as fiction. Chances are that it may come out as a factual experience. But we'll determine that at the proper time. For now, you and Angie are being prepared on the inner for this new venture."*

"I think I've got a lot to talk about with you. I've written a number of books since I wrote *Healing with Padre Pio*, covering a lot of ground; in fact, so much ground that I'm looking forward to exploring new spiritual horizons. I seem to be standing on the edge these days, an edge of intellectual aridity and I need spiritual nurture badly. I've explored a lot of writers and thinkers since *Healing with Padre Pio,* and I'm in desperate need of fresh material; is that why you nudged Penny to go to Orillia Saturday morning, so I could connect with Angie and talk about a sequel to my novel with you?"

"You are ready for a sequel because you are on the edge of intellectual aridity, and our sequel will give you what you need to nurture your spirit."

"So, it's likely that this may happen in the spring, given that I won't finish editing my book of stories and novel until then?"

"Yes. It will take you all winter and then some to complete these books. But they must be out because they will launch you into the literary world of creative writing. I promise you."

"No need for promises, Padre. I know what I have to do, and where the chips fall they will fall; and there's not much I can do about it, is there?'

"As I've told you many times, put your trust in God. It will happen."

"Be that as it may, I just finished editing my story "Our Little Getaway" this morning and I'm very pleased with it. I had Penny read it yesterday, and she likes it very much; and tomorrow morning I'm going to post it on my spiritual musings blog."

"And it will be well-received, I assure you."

"I hope so. Now I'm working on "Kimberly's Gift," and I'm going to be very emotional editing it because it's a deeply personal story. I dread working on it."

"Yes, it is very emotional; but it is also one of your best stories, and it will be read by millions of readers over the years. This I can assure you. This is going to be one of your most anthologized stories."

"Are you serious?"

"I couldn't be more serious. This story will define you."

"As a creative writer?"

"As a writer, period."

"But I won't be alive to see it, though; will I?"

"You will catch the first wave of your recognition. The second wave will come after you cross over, and your name will be around for a long, long time."

"Okay, Padre; I'm too excited. Let's call it a day."

"Fair enough. Take the day off and do what you feel like doing and tomorrow morning you can start fresh on 'Kimberly's Gift.' Until we talk again, my friend…"

11. New Year: 2017

"Good morning, Padre. Today is the first day of the New Year, and I feel like I'm in a fog; maybe because I didn't sleep very well because of my dreams (I don't feel rested, I feel restless), but I'd like to talk with you just to loosen up my creative muscles. Let me start by telling you that I got eleven books from my Amazon wish list for Christmas, which Penny gave me with love (she knows how happy new books make me feel), and I've already read two books completely (*Max Perkins, Editor of Genius* by A. Scott Berg and *A Jungian Life* by Thomas B. Kirsch), and I'm partially into several other books, a lovely, lovely Christmas gift; and I also got a soft brown leather Indigo *Hemingway Notebook* from Penny's sister, which I've already begun to use with the idea of writing a whole book of stories with the working title *Hemingway's Forgotten Notebook,* and in which I have been taking notes for my cover story—which may change, I don't know yet. But I want to talk about this business of story writing, because I've been researching Joyce Carol Oates these past few days and I just don't know what to make of her. Because I chanced upon a YouTube interview of Joyce Carol Oates who read her story "Lovely, Dark, Deep," which by coincidence I had read three years ago in Harper's magazine, which moved me very much because I saw it as frighteningly accurate portrait of Robert Frost's dark side, I became fascinated by Joyce Carol Oates, and I researched her online for a whole week, and more, and I have put several of her books on my Amazon wish list because I feel I have to read her to give me the encouragement I need for my own story writing. What do you think of this, Padre?"

"I think you're onto something. Joyce Carol Oates will be a good role model for writing. She can teach you more about story writing than anybody else, and I highly recommend that you pursue your study of her writing while reading her books. She brings

together everything you need to know about the creative process of writing short stories and novels."

"What makes her such a great and prolific writer?"

"Her love of writing. Love proliferates. That is the simple answer. She works hard. Harder than most writers. She's always thinking about her writing, and always writing. She never loses a minute in her life. It's all about writing. Everything in her life is turned into writing. She has the gift of making up stories from daily insights. That's what she's going to teach you."

"I think I've told you about my visit with Angie, the medium who channeled you for my novel *Healing with Padre Pio*; well, it looks like I may be doing a sequel. Probably in the spring through summer. Is this going to happen?"

"Yes, it will happen; but the time is not set yet."

"Good. I look forward to it. I have lots to work out with you. But is this book going to be fact or fiction?"

"That still remains to be seen."

"How much of an influence will Joyce Carol Oates have on my story writing?"

"Her influence will be obvious and invaluable. She will open up your creative parameters and you will discover whole new worlds to write about in between the spaces, as the phrase goes; and you will learn to write stories not in the first person, which I can't wait to read."

"What do you think of my *Hemingway's Forgotten Notebooks* project?"

"This is the beginning of a whole new way of writing, combining the factual and the fictional in a whole new way. It's going to be an exciting book of stories. Keep working on it as you work on your book Sparkles in the Mist.*"*

"I guess I have to sit firmly on my own talent, my own perspective, my own voice, and learn what I can about story writing so I can write my stories from my unique vantage point. That's the theme of my story 'Hemingway's Forgotten Notebooks.'"

"Yes, and it is a perspective that needs to be out there."

"Okay, Padre; I have to get to work. But first I'm going to post a poem on Facebook in the guise of my New Year's resolution."

A Sign of Things to Come

"It will make your social media friends think. A good poem for 2017."

"Until we talk again…"

12. My Hemingway Notebook

Thursday, January 5, 2017

"Good morning, Padre. I'm just in from shovelling our driveway and I'm a little pooped, so I'm going to work my way slowly into our little chat this morning, if you don't mind."

"Not at all. You do yourself good by doing your driveway. You need more exercise to keep your heart muscle working efficiently. I suggest riding the indoor bike if you cannot get out for a walk. Walking would be better, but do one or both for your heart's sake."

"I have to tell you off the top that I got an Indigo Hemingway Notebook from Penny's young sister for Christmas and that same day I jotted down an idea for a short story, but the idea morphed into the concept of a whole book of stories with the title *Hemingway's Notebooks*, and I'm happy to tell you that I just finished writing the story "Hemingway's Forgotten Notebooks" two days ago and I'd like to know what you think of this idea for a whole new book and my title story. I felt called to write this new book of short stories; but I'm leery."

"Don't be. You have evolved into your own style with your Hemingway story, a style that speaks for those who seek to know the mystery of life. I won't say any more for now. I strongly recommend that you get on with these stories, but only after you have completed Sparkles in the Mist. *You will be given ideas for your* Hemingway's Notebooks *book."*

"Padre, I'm going downstairs to have some toast and plum preserves that Penny and I made last summer. Until later, if you don't mind."

"Enjoy..."

"A day later, but I'm back. I wasn't up to chatting anymore yesterday. I cleaned the ashes out of our wood stove, had my toast and plum preserves, and then I sat in front of the cozy fire and started reading Professor Bloom's book *The Daemon Knows*. I read his chapter on Emily Dickinson, and I marvel at his brilliance but am disappointed that he misses the central genius of her poetry, which is her gnostic awareness of the way. But I'm happy to say that I have implied this in my story "Hemingway's Forgotten Notebooks" that I just finished writing. In fact, I just re-read and edited it again this morning, and I like it. Yesterday you said you couldn't say any more about my story; how about today?"

"Yes, I can say more on the subject. Your story breaks new ground in literature. It opens up the avenue of mystery that all writers seek in their writing. Writers like your new champion Joyce Carol Oates work assiduously to make sense of life through writing, especially her stories and novels, and you have parted the veil of life with your story. She will read it when it comes out. In fact, you should follow up on your thought and send her a copy. Who knows where that will lead."

"I'm not so sure about that. Perhaps after I complete the whole book, then I can send her a copy; but I don't think before that. I need full confidence in my book before I do anything so foolish. I've been down this road before, and I have always regretted it."

"You have come a long way since then, my friend. But do what you feel best."

"I've been given an idea for my next story, but I dread writing it."

"As I suggested, finish you other book of stories first; your book Sparkles in the Mist. *That book has to be out first. Work on it. It will be done quickly if you get down to it."*

"I know. I've been putting it off because the last two stories are too close to home."

"But they are two of your best stories. Just do it. Let your emotions overwhelm you. It will do you good to go back there and re-experience that time of your life."

"You're good to me, Padre. Are you positive through and through?"

"What else would you expect me to be?"

"What a nice way to be. But this doesn't mean you don't see the negative. All it means to me is that you always, always, always accent the positive. Correct?"

"Absolutely."

33

"May I ask you something now so I can have it on record?"

"Ask."

"When we get together with the psychic who will be channeling you, I'm going to explore the hidden part of the iceberg with you, what you told me wasn't mine to explore at the time because I wasn't ready, what you said belonged to the inner workings of the universe; but I feel I've come a long way since I wrote *Healing with Padre Pio,* and I want to know now if you will initiate me into the inner workings of the universe, like parallel lives which I feel is a much deeper reality than I have caught a glimpse of and which speaks to reincarnation in an entirely new way. Are we going to go there?"

"Yes, and much more. But leave that for now. You have other books to get out first. In the early or late summer, or whenever Divine Spirit calls, we will begin our sequel to Healing with Padre Pio, *which may or may not be a novel. That is yet to be determined."*

"Fair enough. Anything else you would like to tell me today?"

"Work on your story 'Kimberly's Gift.' Put in a couple of hours to get some momentum. Once you get into it, you will want to finish it."

"Good. Thank you. Until we talk again, then."

"Ciao for now, my friend..."

13. Author Tom Harpur Dies

"Good morning, Padre. I just read in today's *Saturday Star* that the author of *The Pagan Christ*, Tom Harpur, passed away on *January 2, 2017*. I mention this because his name came up when I wrote *Healing with Padre Pio*. I had read several of his books before I read his highly controversial book *The Pagan Christ,* and as exciting as he was to read, I didn't agree with him on a number of issues, like his non-belief in reincarnation—which, in *The Pagan Christ* he warms up to but cannot quite embrace. And when I brought him up in one of my spiritual healing sessions with the psychic medium who was channeling you, you told me that Tom Harpur was confused. He had a lot of information, but all of this information had confused him, and he came to the erroneous conclusion that Jesus the man did not exist as a historical person. I had no trouble believing you, because I have no doubt that Jesus did exist. And in a later spiritual healing session you suggested that I read the book *Love without End, Jesus Speaks*, by Glenda Green, which I did; and it was one of the most satisfying books I ever read, because in this book Jesus appears to Glenda Green to paint his portrait, and while painting his portrait Jesus fills in the gaps of his teaching that can't be found in the New Testament Gospels. Now that Tom Harpur is on the other side, I wonder how he feels about his belief in Jesus. Any thoughts, Padre?"

"Like yourself, he was on his own journey. A soul's journey is individual, and it depends upon how one exercises his free will that determines the nature of their journey. Tom Harpur exercised his free will in a direction that led him to much confusion, and in his confusion, he drew conclusions that were not real. Your free will brought you to your true self; and in your journey, you experienced the reality of your higher nature. That's the difference between you and the author of The Pagan Christ. You are the author of many books that speak to your truth, as he is the author of many books that speak to his truth. It's up to every soul to choose which truth they are

most comfortable with. I am pleased with the books that you wrote. They resonate with me."

"Speaking of my books, I just tightened up my story 'Hemingway's Forgotten Notebooks' this morning, and then I posted my poem "An Island in the Middle of Manhattan" on my Spiritual Musings blog, and then I checked out my manuscript *Enantiodromia* just to see what I should do with it, and I do have to write a novella titled 'The Funeral Service' to complete this book of stories, but I don't know when I can get to it. I've got my hands full with *Sparkles in the Mist*, but I hope to get to it eventually. I also want to edit and tighten up my novel *An Atheist, An Agnostic, and Me*; but I don't know if I can get to it before spring."

"This is a very important novel for you. You have to polish it and get it out there, because it will fill in many gaps in your life story."

"Okay, what about my novel *Cathedral of My Past Lives*?"

"Another novel that you have to get out. It is one of your more important books, if not the most important. That will be determined by your readers."

"And my novel based on my open-heart surgery, *The Sweet Breath of Life*?"

"You see the work that you have ahead of you? So, don't waste any time and get your work out there. You have much written that needs to be polished and published. I know you are called to new books, but you have to learn to use your time productively."

"I know, and my time is getting thinner and thinner."

"You will get out what you have written, and much more."

"Thank you for that. Until we talk again, then."

"Have a productive day, my friend..."

14. Down with a Cold

Tuesday, January 24, 2017

"I'm in a strange place again, not only because of my cold and coughing, which isn't as bad as I thought it would be because when I start coughing I feel like it's going to grab hold of me and not let go, and I know that when I die it'll probably be because of TB and/or pneumonia, but that's not going to be for a while because I have ten more books to write before I go; but I do have some issues to discuss with you, especially my feelings about Professor Harold Bloom whose extraordinary gift for literary criticism baffles me. I have to ask you something about his preternatural gift for reading and his unbelievable memory. He was born with these gifts, and he attributes them to some genetic inheritance; but I suspect something more. I believe that his daemonic genius speaks to the spirit of literature. I can't express it any other way for now, but I'd like to know if you agree with how I feel about his genius. I feel that his daemon possessed him at an early age to speak for the spirit of literature—which is not enough to free soul from life, and this is why Professor Bloom is so melancholic. He makes my heart heavy."

"Professor Harold Bloom is an extraordinary man who will not be appreciated in his lifetime the way his genius should be appreciated, but he knows this and has given up on the world catching up to him; but you have caught the essence of the man's spirit. His daemon possessed him early, and he was off to the races. His daemon is unique in the history of the world. He does speak for the spirit of literature, but as you have come to see, literature is not enough to free man's soul from the endless cycle of life and death; and what you have in Professor Bloom is the ecstasy and sadness of man's becoming but never being what he is meant to be, whole and complete. This is why he makes your heart heavy and why you have so much love and respect for him. He is a tragic man who cannot resolve the issue of the human condition through literature, and the failure of literature is his personal tragedy."

"I'm scared, Padre. I'm scared to write. That's why I've been putting it off. I'm scared because I'm having a crisis of confidence. I don't think I'm good enough to write the stories I have to write to feel the way I want to feel when I get them written, if you know what I mean."

"It's only natural to feel afraid as you read the best writers. You are pitting yourself with the very best, but you have a talent they do not possess: you found the way. That makes you one of the fortunate few who can write about the way consciously and not unconsciously or semi-consciously as most writers do. Don't fret. Rely upon your own talent and build upon it. It will take you where you need to go with ever story that you write."

"What do you suggest for how I can consolidate my energies? I feel like I have to get my energies to come together into one focus. How can I do that?"

"That's the mystery of creative genius, when one's talent is focused with such intensity that it burns a hole through life's condition and sets soul free. That's what Professor Bloom calls the American Sublime. You have achieved this in your writing, and you will achieve it again. Rest up for a few more days, and in the meantime read lightly and drink plenty of fluids; and sometime in the next few days you will get the inspiration you need to consolidate your energies, and you will harness your talent and complete the books you have started. Now get something to eat and rest in front of the fire and try to read more and watch less TV."

"Will do…"

15. Keeping a Journal, of a Sort

"Padre, I'd like to write something every morning to get my day started. Keeping a journal, of a sort, but with feedback from you; if that's okay?"

"By all means. It would be like priming the pump to get the flow going."

"I feel I've lost the art of journal writing. I used to do it all the time, and it felt good to dive into the deep of my life without thought or reservation. It always got me to the deep waters of the creative energy of life without that much effort, and I'd like to begin again because I'm getting very tired and bored of my life being so routinely unproductive. I know I've written a new story and started a new one, but it's not flowing like I would like it to, and I think that by tapping into the deep well of my creative life I will get back into that flow I was used to. I've been watching a lot of news lately, following the Trump election and his presidency and loving every minute because he's shaking up the system, but the truth is Padre, I'm just avoiding what I'm supposed to be doing—WRITING!"

"Not that it's not important to keep up with world events, they inform your writing, but you are right; you do avoid your literary calling. But perhaps this exercise in journaling will tap you deeply into the creative spring of life and you will re-establish your habit."

"I'd like nothing more than to be possessed by my creative daemon again. Can you tell me how else I can reconnect with my daemon besides this type of journal writing?"

"The answer is simple: the more you write the more you will want to write. Journal writing like this begins the process and keeps it alive. Just do what you are doing and let it flow into your story writing. And if you feel tired with lack of energy, sit back and wait a few minutes and get right back into it. You will reconnect, I promise."

"There's another thing I want to run by you. As I said, I've been following the news a lot lately, which keeps me abreast of world events, but the avoidance of my writing leaves me feeling guilty. In my defense, I've come to see the superficiality of life as it flows past me on the television screen as I watch the news of the world, especially in the US and Canada, and I'm left wondering what the hell is going on out there. Can I ask you this simple, blunt question?"

"The universe is unfolding as it should. You need not concern yourself with the turn of world events. You have a good insight on the process now. Trust your instincts. You know why soul is here, and it doesn't matter how soul learns its lessons; learn them, soul will; all you have to do is record your journey, because your journey tells the story of one's soul's liberation from the eternal process of soul's becoming. You ARE, and all you have to do is BE who you ARE. Write your stories and let the world unfold accordingly. Don't fret over conditions. As you wisely surmised, providence and free will work together; and that's how it's meant to be."

"I've been concerned about focusing my energies lately, like I've spread myself too thin to do any serious writing; but I think I've solved this with this type of journal writing. I do believe I may just prime my pump every morning with a daily entry. I hope you don't mind."

"If I can be of any service for your writing, by all means."

"Well, I've started another story. My working title was 'The Full but Incomplete Life,' but I changed it to 'The Art Perfects.' What do you think of my story so far?"

"I like both titles, but for literary reasons I would select the latter. Your story is going very well. It's only started. You have a way to go yet, but you will get there; and it will be true to the theme of your first story and your book, which reveals the secret way of life as you have experienced it. Your stories will let the reader into the secret."

"Was that the purpose of my new book of stories?"

"Yes. Hemingway's Forgotten Notebooks *will be a wonderful book of stories. It will be more of a novel-like book of related stories, and that will please the reader."*

"I have a feeling I may be exploring some very deep, personal experiences in this book, and I'm going to need all the encouragement I can get because I hate to go back to those experiences. Once was enough for me, thank you. Will you be there for me?"

A Sign of Things to Come

"Of course. I may even suggest a story or two for you."

"I've made a discovery about *story* and the secret way that I want to explore in my story writing, because the secret way of life is our own individuation process, is it not?"

"Yes. This is the connective theme of Hemingway's Forgotten Notebooks. *You will write a story for each of your experiences with the way as you lived it, letting the reader into the mystery deeper and deeper with each story. This is a pivotal book for you, and you will realize this as you get deeper into it. Once you complete your second story, you will know."*

"Should I follow up on my study of Joyce Carol Oates?"

"Yes. She will do you a world of good."

"And is Professor Bloom working on his new book, which he thinks he's going to call *Possessed by Memory*? It may change by the time he's finished, but I hope he completes it before passing on. He's in his mid-eighties, and his health isn't the best."

"He will complete it, but barely. It is a big book about his life. You will love it."

"How come the world is so slow to catch on to him?"

"How come the world is so slow to catch on to your hero Doctor C. G. Jung?"

"People don't want to know the answer to life's big questions. They want formulas for quick solutions to their problems; that's what I've come to see."

"And you wouldn't be wrong. Like Professor Bloom and Doctor Jung, you also are out of step with society; but that's no reason to be discouraged. Just do what you have been called to do, and let the world find its own way to Bloom, Jung, and you."

"Please, let me just be me without the vainglory."

"You've long overgrown vainglory. You're on the home stretch now."

"Good. I need a rest from all that nonsense."

"True enough, but remember: without it you wouldn't be here. We are our own story, and if our story gets us to where we are supposed to be, who can question the story?"

"I guess the point of my story-writing has to do with how to get to where one is supposed to go when one's story gets interrupted, or something to that effect."

"Yes. And much more."

"What do you mean?"

"That's the surprise element of creative writing. You must write to find out."

"Fair enough. Thank you, Padre. Until tomorrow, then."

"Ciao for now, my friend..."

16. The Labyrinth of the Mind

Sunday, January 29, 2017

"I got up late this morning, a little after six, and didn't want to get out of bed; but I did, got dressed, went downstairs, put coffee on, rekindled the fire from the coals, poured myself a cup of coffee, and dipped into *The Daemon Knows* by the magnificent professor Bloom; but then I decided to come upstairs to write instead. It snowed yesterday, and the driveway needs to be plowed; but I don't think there's enough snow to use the blower. I'll go out later, or Penny will and do it by hand. I hope I get to do it before Penny does so I can get some exercise. I'm not into exercise these days, and I should be; but let's leave that for now. I noticed as I was reading Bloom's chapter on Ralph Waldo Emerson that his favorite poet Hart Crane had read the man whom professor Bloom called "the unreadable P. D. Ouspensky," and I wondered how much Crane had read about Gurdjieff's teaching, and how far he took it. Was that the source of his esotericism? I could order his biography and find out, but would it be necessary? I can't get into Crane's poetry, and I wonder if it would be worth my bother. But Bloom certainly has been possessed by him. Last night I couldn't get Bloom out of my mind as I tried to fall asleep. I wondered if his soul was stuck in a pattern of eternal return, which might explain his unbelievable memory. He's so amazing in his memory that he's frightening, and I wonder if his memory hasn't driven him close to madness; but I'd like to ask you Padre, what about the concept of eternal return? Could his soul be in a pattern of returning to the same life over and over again because he's stuck in his beliefs? Is that why he loves Nietzsche? Is that kind of reincarnation possible?"

"It is, and you have just penetrated the mystery about professor Bloom's phenomenal memory and preternatural reading ability. He's stuck in an eternal pattern of the one life that he has taken to extreme limits, and not until he finds a way out of the labyrinth of his mind will he move on to another pattern of reincarnation. But we will talk about this more with the medium."

"I'm quickly coming to realize that as much as science knows about the mind and body, it knows practically nothing about the soul; this is what bothers me about professor Bloom. His breathtaking knowledge of literature should have given him a way out of the labyrinth of his own mind, but it hasn't. He's deep into the melancholic hold of his despairing nihilism."

"Why do you think he called Ouspensky unreadable, and why do you think he got headaches when he taught Emily Dickinson's poetry? He refuses to go where he knows in his soul he must go to free himself from the labyrinth of his great mind."

"So, reincarnation? Linear, parallel, and eternal return? What more?"

"This will be a good portion of your new book with me when we get together through your medium next summer or the year after. I look forward to it."

"You know, Padre; I'm glad I was compelled to write my twin soul books. I think these books will define my career as a seeker. *Death, the Final Frontier* and *The Merciful Law of Divine Synchronicity* are my two most succinct books on the *way*, wouldn't you say?"

"They certainly go a long way to explaining what the way is, and you should be very proud of them. Yes, they will define your career as a seeker of truth, and they will do much more for your writing because they will open doors to new horizons once the readers start reading them. You will be given many benefits from the freedom you allow your readers with these books. This is how the merciful law of divine karma works."

"The more freedom one gives, the more one receives? Is that what you mean?"

"Yes."

"This leads me to the question of the karma-free life. I'm almost there, aren't I?"

"Very much so. And we will be talking about this in our new book."

"I feel like a man apart, just as I feel professor Bloom is a man apart, and my hero C. G. Jung, and the poet Emily Dickinson. We are souls apart, aren't we?"

A Sign of Things to Come

"Yes. You have all taken your own path, and you each serve your purpose in the evolution of social consciousness. This is as it should be."

"Why is professor Bloom afraid to explore the secret way of life?"

"He does so through literature, but he cannot walk through the door to the other side of life that literature offers, and by other side I mean the mystic path that the way demands of its seekers. You walked through that door, and you know what it costs. Professor Bloom does not want to pay the price. He is much too large to sacrifice his life for the secret way. That is his pattern that he must break free of, but it will take much greater despair than he is suffering in the melancholy of his great mind before he steps through that door. 'Strait is the gate, and narrow is the way, which leadeth unto life, and few there be that find it.' This is the tragic mystery of eternal recurrence. Ouspensky had a great mind also, and he believed in the eternal recurrence of the soul. As you know, he wrote a novel on eternal recurrence; that's why he never made the progress that he hoped to make in his journey to what Jesus called 'the pearl of great price.' You did, so you know the price one has to pay. Your friend Alice paid this price with her life. Sad, but glorious. You did her life proud, my friend. The Pearl of Great Price will one day become a classic."

"Thank you. I hope to also write a novella on my experience with Alice. I had a working title, 'The Funeral Service,' but I got nudged to change it to 'The Elephant in the Room.' I hope I get to write it. It will be the story of my experience with that New Age teaching that I lived all those years before I met you through the medium who channeled you for my novel *Healing with Padre Pio*. I'm so glad I met you, Padre. You spared me a lot of grief with your compassion and understanding. I will be forever grateful."

"You were ready to move on, and you needed a little shove. And now that you are here, you can write about your experience with a knowledge and detachment that will do your story justice. I cannot wait for this story to be written. And I love your new title."

"Padre, I'm going online to do some research on the American poet Hart Crane. Thank you for the chat this morning. Until we talk again."

"Be kind to him, my friend."

"Who? Hart Crane?"

"Yes."

"His life, his karma."

"True. But be kind all the same. His light burnt bright, and his poetry will never die."

"Is that professor Bloom's fascination with his poetry, the incandescent light of his tortured soul? Is that what attracted him to Hart Crane when he was only ten or twelve years old?"

"Professor Bloom was possessed by the daemonic spirit of literature, that's why he was compelled to write his ground-breaking book The Anxiety of Influence; *but that's a story for another time. Do your research, but bear in mind that all writers drink from the same fountain, and you have much more in common than you realize."*

"Yes, I know; a writer is a writer, and we all look for the way out of Plato's cave. Crane got lost in the shadows, that's all I meant to say."

"Fair enough, my friend..."

17. Feeling Overwhelmed Again

Monday, January 30, 2017

"Here I am again, Padre; feeling overwhelmed by my life, as though tomorrow will be a burden of boredom if I don't do something today to overcome my feelings of inadequacy. Maybe I've been doing too much Bloom for my own good, getting overwhelmed by his sense of nihilism that has doomed him to perpetual despair, and I should stop reading him and move on to my own work which reflects the meaning and purpose of my life that I sought for and found in my own becoming, which brought me to you and new vistas of understanding. But who cares? That's the feeling that pervades me this morning, who cares? All of this writing is for naught, is it not? And if you say it's not, it sure feels like it. If only I could know for certain!"

"You do know for certain, as one of your readers in England has proven. He read your book on Gurdjieff's teaching and the effect it had on you, and it proved to be very helpful in his own search. He was stuck, and your book got him out of his dilemma, and he's not the only reader. Every reader of your books will feel a sense of freedom they never had before, because your writing liberates the soul from the mind. That's the gift of your writing."

"I'm never more doubtful of myself than when I'm not writing. If only I could stick to one project and get it finished I'd be a happy man!"

"What's stopping you?"

"Fear of failure? Fear of talent? Fear of craftsmanship?"

"Fear of your muse. Fear of your daemon. Fear of your own talent. You have opened up the door to your higher intelligence, and you fear stepping in. Just write and let it flow. That's what the great writers do. Trust yourself, my friend."

"I came upon an interesting insight the other day. Faulkner described Thomas Wolfe as being 'extinguished by the divine fire.'

One could say that of Hart Crane as well, and probably Keats and Shelly also. Could they not handle the Holy Flame of God?"

"It burned them out early. The Holy Flame of God scorches the soul, and few souls have the strength to withstand it's cleansing. You did. You survived the madness that could have possessed you, but you fought your battle and you won your battle; and now you must write your story in all of its ecstasy and glory. Just write, my friend; just write."

"I rekindled the fire this morning, but we are almost out of firewood. We have enough for another few days, so I have to order some more; and I put on the coffee pot and read some Dickinson this morning, and I became overwhelmed by that feeling of inadequacy, that's why I came to my computer to chat with you, so I could get some balance and make my day worthwhile with honest effort and endeavor. I do need your assistance, though."

"And you have it."

"I just wish I could satisfactorily answer the question WHO CARES? That really bothers me, because I see myself being irrelevant in the grand scheme of things. The world is moving fast according to its own seemingly insane rhythm, and I seem helpless to add some clarity to this confusion; that's why I feel helpless to the situation. What could I possibly say that would add some understanding and meaning to this confusing world? Our new American President Donald Trump seems to have opened up a Pandora's Box with his executive orders, like refusing to let immigrants in from seven countries—implying racism. People are protesting, and it seems like this may be more than what he expected. What's going on out there, Padre?"

"As you say, the world is unfolding according to its own rhythm, and there's not much anyone can do about it but try to understand. Don't fret, my friend; this is a new world that is opening up, and much is yet to come that will free man from his slumber. This is the purpose of his presidency, to wake the world up to the reality of the situation. He will do more good than even he will ever realize, because he was chosen by the spirit of the times to set the world on a different course. It was stuck, and he was called to set it free from its mindsets."

"And personally, how safe and secure should I feel?"

A Sign of Things to Come

"You are in God's hands, my friend. You are safe and secure and loved. Feel free to do what you were called to do, and write your stories."

"I sure wish we could sell our triplex."

"The door has been opened, and soon you will be free of that responsibility."

"My new book of stories, *Hemingway's Forgotten Notebooks,* I feel like it wants to pull me to that place I don't want to go to, but I must; right?"

"Yes."

"Okay. Thank you for the encouragement. I can always trust you to lift my spirits. I'm going to get on with my day, and please give me a shove when I need it."

"I will..."

18. River of Karma

Tuesday, February 21, 2017

"Good morning, Padre. Penny and I went to Barrie last Sunday for a movie and dinner; but when we came out of the Uptown Theatre where we watched *Manchester by the Sea*, we weren't very happy, because that movie was oppressive and depressing. Penny wanted to walk out ten minutes into the movie, and this colored the rest of the day for us, spoiling our dinner at Wimpy's Diner. We had a simple hot hamburger and an order of onion rings, but it didn't taste as good as it should have had we not been colored by *Manchester by the Sea*. I said to Penny that it was like watching a river of karma, sweeping all the characters down the river of their own making, and it was depressing watching how they became victims of their own unfortunate choices; but you know what, Padre? I'm seeing that every day on the news now. I can't believe how clearly I'm seeing the fixed states of consciousness that keep people victims of their own shadow. What's going on with me? Am I so far removed now that I can see the river of karma flowing through life, sweeping souls down the river of their own making?"

"That's a good metaphor. Yes, you are more removed now than ever before, and you are watching karma in action; but you have not yet adjusted to your new perspective. You will see much more clearly soon enough, and you will understand what I meant by the karma-free life. It's all a question of consciousness and self-awareness."

"And the courage to be true to oneself when one becomes aware of his/her own falseness, which most people don't have; that's why they look so foolish when they get caught in their self-deceptions, which I've been witnessing daily as I watch the news. Journalists who fail to admit that they are wrong in their understanding and stick to their ideology instead of going with the reality of the situation. It's bizarre!"

"Very bizarre. But that's human nature."

A Sign of Things to Come

"I wrote a new first chapter for my book *The Merciful Law of Divine Synchronicity*. Penny said it needed something to make the story come alive, more synchronicities; so I wrote a whole new chapter that gives the pattern of the story on how the merciful law of synchronicity comes into play in our life to bring our karmic destiny into alignment with our spiritual destiny, and I'm glad that Penny suggested it. It does the story justice; don't you think?"

"Yes. It was exactly what your story needed. Now your reader can make the connection that otherwise would have been too elusive. It makes your story real and believable."

"And I think we're going to publish this next. I was thinking of publishing my book of poetry, *Not My Circus, Not My Monkeys*; but I've changed my mind. I want my twin soul book *The Merciful Law of Divine Synchronicity* out next."

"I agree. Keep your twin soul books together."

"I'm getting ideas for my new book of short stories, *Hemingway's Forgotten Notebooks*, three or four ideas now, and I even started one the other day, "The Snow Blower," but I can't seem to get down to business; I'm pulled this way and that and can't get into my new stories. But I did edit my story "Brussels Sprout." I may post this one on my blog next weekend."

"It's a good little story. It will open up a lot of minds to the idea of reincarnation. Yes, by all means; get it out on your blog, and then complete your other stories and try to have this book out by next summer. It's important that you do."

"Why?"

"The more you publish, the more freedom you will have to write new stories. This is how the river of your own karma works for you. Much gathers more, as it were."

"I've still got my fourth volume of spiritual musings, *The Armchair Guru*, to put out. I have to write the conclusion to one musing still, and then I can edit and get it out; but I seem to be putting this book off for one reason or another. But I want it out this coming summer."

"Good. Then you can start on your fifth volume of spiritual musings. I know you are itching to write more spiritual musings, and by the time you get The Armchair Guru *out you will be ready to write*

new musings; only this time they will be more pertinent, and more reader friendly."

"You think so?"

"I know so, my friend. I see it here already. But you have four or five books to publish before you get your fifth volume of spiritual musings ready."

"And are we going to work on a new book together with the medium who channeled you for my novel *Healing with Padre Pio?"*

"Yes. This will be another novel, although you may decide otherwise. The choice is open."

"I suspect it will be another novel like the former. The transcripts will be what we talk about in our sessions, and the chapters in between will be fictionalized."

"Yes. It may very well be. That will be up to you."

"I'm curious to see how you respond to my inquiry about my dialectic with you in my writing and our discussions with you and the medium. That should be interesting."

"Why? Don't you trust your own superior insight?"

"I don't know what to trust. I'm in a strange place. And speaking of strange places, I've been down the rabbit hole of my own idiocy this past few weeks, and I hate myself for it."

"Move on, my friend. We all fall into rabbit holes in life. Tomorrow is another day, and try not to step into rabbit holes on your way to more life and love."

"Thank you. I can get on with my day now. I'm going to read and tighten my story "Brussels Sprout" so I can have it ready for my blog this coming weekend."

"Happy writing…"

19. The Mote in the Eye

Sunday, February 26, 2017

"Dare I say it, Padre? I like Donald Trump, the President of the United States who is loathed, reviled, hated, and detested by many people who call him a racist, misogynist, narcissist, and many other names that one cannot mention; but why is he hated so much? I thought about this for a long time, and this morning something Jesus said came to mind: *"And why beholdest thou the mote that is in thy brother's eye, but considerest not the beam that is in thine own eye?"* In therapy known as 'shadow work', one must learn to see that what one hates in another person's character lies deep within their own character; does this mean that all those people who hate Donald Trump don't have the courage to face up to their own shadow? How's that for an opening remark? Do you care to comment, Padre?"

"You got your answer in Christ's words. President Trump has a knack for raising the hackles of the un-self-realized. The less conscious one is of their shadow, the more they dislike the President of the United States. His genius is his egoic nature. He is himself within all of his contradictions, and people are afraid of him because he dares to be himself in all of his contradictions, whether he is aware of them or not. He dares to risk being himself, and this terrifies people. President Trump puzzles the world because a man full of contradictions cannot be boxed in and predicted. He's free to act within the parameters of his own person, which on the whole is a good person who wants to do good for his country."

"He's awakened the shadow of the American psyche, and the shadow does not like what it sees; is that it?"

"Well put. But America had better get used to it, because he's going to be there for a while and he will change the course of America's history."

"I believe he will also. In fact, I feel he was chosen by the better nature of the American people to help set America free from the stranglehold of its shadow. In fact, I had a vision of former President Obama choking a woman, which to me symbolized the choke-hold that his administration had upon America; and I feel that Trump is going to release this choke-hold so America can breathe freely again."

"That was an accurate image. You have been initiated into the deeper mysteries of life's narrative, and you will be seeing more of this narrative unfold in ways that no-one else will because you are outside the box of conventional thought and see things differently. Keep a record of what you see in our talks. It will prove interesting reading down the road."

"I will. Okay, on to something else. Yesterday morning Penny and I went over her edits of my book *The Merciful Law of Divine Synchronicity,* and I can't wait to get it out. Once she formats and uploads it onto Lulu, she can order two proof copies; and then we can do our final proof and get it published and on Amazon. I'm glad I wrote my twin soul books, Padre; they seem to sum up my journey of self-discovery very nicely. I only wish I could get into my story writing with the emotional intensity that I wrote my twin soul books. I miss that creative intensity. I edited my story "Brussels Sprout" and am ready for Penny to read it, but I'm leery about her reading it because it's pretty close to home. I hope it doesn't upset her."

"No, it will not upset her. It will give her an insight into your life that she will appreciate much more than she already does. Trust her judgment."

"Will I ever get my emotional creative intensity back again?"

"Not to the degree that you had it, but enough to complete the books that you have to write and get published. Trust yourself. You have enough creative desire to complete your task. Just do it, one story at a time. That's all you need to do. Don't think of anything else. One story at a time and nothing more. Go from story to story to story, and before you know it you will have accomplished everything you want to accomplish. Trust me, my friend."

"I really don't have any choice, do I? After all, what else is there but neglect and despair? I have to struggle along and get it done, one story at a time. But I wish I could get some rhythm into my life, a steady flow of doing and doing and more doing. That's what I wish."

"What's stopping you?"

"My own fears, I guess."

A Sign of Things to Come

"Yes, your fears. But doing overcomes fear. Just write every day. Work on one of your stories every day. That's how you can get into the rhythm you desire."

"Thank you for the inspiration. Until we talk again, then."

"You will find the rhythm of your life as you DO YOUR LIFE; meaning, the more you do what you have been called to do, which is to write, the more you will be in sync with the rhythm of life. That's how you bring your inner and outer life into one synchronized life."

"Okay. I'm going to sign off now. Thank you for your understanding."

"You're welcome..."

20. Want to Run Away...

Wednesday, March 1, 2017

"Here I am again, Padre; with that feeling of wanting to run away, brought on by the loss of one of our tenants, the young couple who occupied the top suite of our triplex for the last two years; now we have to find another tenant. God, I wish we could sell that place."

"It's normal to be anxious, but don't be; your triplex will find its tenant very shortly. You have no need for anxiety because you are in God's hands. This is a fact that is difficult to grasp, not because it's so abstract but because it's too good to believe. When you are in God's hands, everything falls into its proper place. Let me explain this. It's one thing to believe that God is the creator of all that happens in life, but this is not the case because man has free will; and not until man realizes that his will and God's will must be in sync will one appreciate what it means to be in God's hands. You have spent your life bringing your will into agreement with your destined purpose, which is God's purpose; and now that you have found your path, which is to align your will with God's will, you have been firmly grasped by the hand of God. Does this make sense?"

"It does. But still, I'm anxious because I fear the insecurity that comes with the loss of income. I know it's foolish, because we'll manage all the same; but fear is fear, and this has always been my biggest problem. But then, I've had a lot of time to write carefree; and I can be thankful for that. I'd just like to continue writing carefree, and by carefree I mean not having to worry about our triplex and tenants. Can you oversee this for me, please?"

"I can, and will. You must allow the process to work its way into a new rhythm. It will happen very shortly, and you will be in a new writing rhythm as well. You got to see the hectic, if not chaotic life of the writer Thomas Wolfe in the movie 'Genius' that you saw last night, and if you would compare your life to his, what would you say?"

A Sign of Things to Come

"I respect him for his genius, but as a man he was lost; that's why I quoted him for my short story 'Hemingway's Forgotten Notebooks.' Wolfe was looking for the *way*, and he thought he could find it in and through his writing, which is why he was so haunted and driven by his daemon; but I found the *way*, and I am no longer haunted and driven. So, comparatively speaking, he can have his genius and I'll keep my peace of mind."

"And there you have it. So just do what you have to do and let God take care of the rest. You started working on your story 'Kimberly's Gift' this morning, keep typing and get as much done today as you can. It will help to set your new rhythm."

"I also saw another movie yesterday, 'Papa Hemingway in Cuba,' which fascinated me because of my respect for my high school hero and literary mentor; but it wasn't as well done as I would have liked. It was stilted and wooden in many places, but enjoyable nonetheless for the information it gave about this part of Hemingway's life. It also goes to the issue of one's need to find the way through writing. This might just be inspiration for a new spiritual musing. What do you think, Padre; should I give it a shot?"

"You've been meaning to start a new series of spiritual musings. If you think you can pry open the door to that part of your talent, do so. I'll be there for you if you do."

"I have a growing urge to do so. In fact, the title of my musing just came to me—perhaps provided by you, or my creative unconscious?"

"By your creative unconscious, which is trying to tell you something that you have been tuning out lately. You need to get those creative muscles working for you again. Go ahead, spend a few hours on this musing just to see where it will take you. I like the title. It might open up to a whole new perspective on writing, something that you may need to help you complete your book of short stories and your novels. Do it. I'll be right here when you need me."

"Okay, I will. I'll open up a new file. I may call it 'My Writing Life.'"

"It's a good working title."

"Alright, here goes…"

21. Not a Funk, but Something

Friday, April 28, 2017

"Good morning, Padre. I've been putting calling on you for a long time now, except for last night when Penny and I needed your comfort for the little trouble we had with a water leak in the middle apartment of our triplex up north which sent me into panic mode—the kind of panic that makes my heart race and scares the hell out of me; but this morning I'm calling on you because I have to clear up a few things that are coming to a head for me. I hope you don't mind me calling on you this way. I do so need to be listened to. I have no one else I can share this with, and I do feel it's time to get this out of my system, starting with my feelings of anxiety about the whole damn purpose of my writing life. I've written all these books which one day will go into the dustbin and one wonders why all the fuss and bother, and here I am again working on another book about my writing life; what's the point, Padre?"

"The point is to keep you busy, to keep you focussed, to keep you involved in the creative process which will profit those who read your books. They are not written in vain. You may not believe this now, as most writers don't when they feel sorry for themselves as you are doing, but books don't really die; they get put away somewhere in the archives of life and resurface when they are needed, and your books will always be around for people to read when they are ready for the kind of wisdom you have to offer them. You have to keep in mind that your writing is a personal activity, your individual path in life which you worked very hard to realize, and through the act of writing you grow into the soul you have become. This is your destiny."

"What about our house up north? Will it ever sell?"

"Yes. Lower the price to one hundred and fifty-nine thousand and it will sell within weeks on the market. Do this this summer."

"I'd like to, but Penny will object."

A Sign of Things to Come

"Try to reason with her. Work out the numbers and give it a go."

"What about a tenant for our middle apartment?"

"Done."

"Simple as that?"

"Yes."

"And my writing? What about the sequel to *Healing with Padre Pio*? Will I be getting this started this summer? After we get our middle apartment rented?"

"Yes. It is coming. It will be a big event in your life, as well as your medium's life who will channel me for your sequel. This will be a very important book for both of you."

"Will it be in novel form again?"

"Yes. This is the best way for this book to go. A sequel to the original."

"I'm getting whisperings for my novel *We May Be Tiny, But We're Not Small*. I can feel the spirit of this novel sneaking up on me."

"This novel will be your most creative literary novel. It will be written with all the wisdom that you will acquire studying the art of writing that you are doing now. This novel will occupy your time and you will give it more effort than most of your books; and by effort, I mean literary effort like your literary mentor Earnest Hemingway. I look forward to this novel."

"I feel somewhat comforted, but not quite as much as I would like. I'm still in a funk about my life right now, especially with our triplex. I hope we can get a tenant soon and that it will sell this summer and I will try to get Penny to lower the price. But with respect to my life in particular, I'd like to get some of my discipline back. I feel like I'm fraying at the edges."

"I know how you feel. You need inspiration to get you motivated physically. Go for walks this summer. Make a stern habit of it. This will give you the discipline you need to inspire you in other activities. Make the effort. Focus and do it."

"I'll try. Thank you for listening. You do comfort me. I'm still not over my funk, but I do feel better. I've got a lot of stuff already written that I'd like to get out, but I'm called to write other stuff. What do I do?"

"Do what you are called to do. The rest will take care of itself."

"The call, the call, the call—always the bloody call!"

"Yes, my friend; that is the fate of those who are called to their destiny."

"Am I right in believing that my books are ahead of their time?"

"Yes and no. They are ahead of their time insomuch that one has to be made ready by life to appreciate them, but they will inspire those who read them but are not ready. You read many books that you were not ready for, and they gave you some inspiration. Life is not for us to understand. It's for us to live. Life will always work it out for everybody. Just live your life as you have been called to live it and give back to life the wisdom that you have earned, because in the giving you add to the truth and beauty of existence. This is Soul's purpose."

"Okay. That's enough for today. Thank you."

"You're welcome..."

22. Here We Go Again

Thursday, May 18, 2017

"Here we go again, Padre; I'm really, really hating myself for not taking better care of my body. I just caught a glimpse of myself in the mirror and I shuddered in fright at what I saw, the protruding belly and the lump of my—I can't think of the name, but it's got me worried. Why in God's name can't I do something about my health? Please tell me."

"You know what to do, but you are so keen on writing about your journey of self-discovery that you have no energy left for your physical well being. I know it's important that you write about your journey, but it's time to take a break. You do have to get your body in shape, and the place to start is always NOW. Here's my list of tips for you: 1. Drink five to six full glasses of water every day. 2. Drink your Essiac tea daily. 3. Cut back on your eating, especially breads. 4. Do a minimum of thirty minutes of walking or cycling daily. 5. Do some light body exercises to tighten up your body and keep you limber. 6. Drink alcohol very moderately. Make a habit of these six rules and within a month you will see a noticeable difference."

"Okay. I'm starting NOW!

"Good..."

23. Another Book Brought Home

Wednesday, June 14, 2017

"I've been reading my book *The Man of God Walks Alone* every morning for the past week or so and I'm really enjoying my talks with you in this book, and this morning I saw how much I miss talking with you Padre; so if you don't mind, I think I'm going to exercise this privilege I have with you, or is it my superior mind? Whatever it is, it does me good. What do you say?"

"I say it's about time. You have earned the privilege to talk with me and you should take advantage of it, whether it be me or your superior mind, or both. You have to come to your own conclusion about that, which I think you already have; but no matter, just let go and let your creative unconscious speak. This is how you can get to where you want to be."

"Before we go anywhere, please help clear up my apprehensions about our triplex up north. Would you please intervene?"

"I'm working on it. Lower your price and it will sell. Just do it."

"Okay, no more on that subject because I don't want to sound like a whiner. But all of those issues…"

"It's all a matter of course. Don't fret. It's all taken care of. Lower the price and let the marketplace decide. It will, I promise you."

"Alright, now to the question of my new book. I brought it home the other day. Now I'm editing *My Writing Life…* It's my sequel to *The Lion that Swallowed Hemingway*, and I never expected to bring it home the other night; but there I was, talking with Penny after her sister, who was visiting us for several days, went to bed, and as we talked I read the last paragraph of the last chapter that I had just written and I *knew* that that was the end of the book, and a great relief washed over me. What do you think of my sequel to my Hemingway book?"

A Sign of Things to Come

"You surprised yourself. Yes, it was a great relief for you because you finally came to a satisfactory resolution with your relationship with Ernest Hemingway. You had to write that book to get Hemingway out of your system. Now you can move on to your own writing. And yes, I like the book very much. It speaks to the secret way of life in literature, and that is no mean accomplishment. You have opened the door for many readers to see the real value of poetry and literature, and for this you will be greatly appreciated and rewarded."

"I gave Penny my book of poetry *Not My Circus, Not My Monkeys* to read and edit and format for publishing, so we should have that out in a month or so; and I'm editing my book *My Writing Life* that I just brought to closure and hope to have out after my poetry book, and then I have to get back to *Sparkles in the Mist* because I can't put this one off any longer. I do get diverted from one project to another, but I seem to get to where I have to be, don't I?"

"Well put. Yes, you do get there eventually; and look at what you produce while you are getting there. This is your pattern, and it's not a bad one. Just keep doing what you are doing and let your muse guide you. It's a good place to be for a writer."

"I have demon fears creeping into my mind—"

"Don't fret. Your demon fears are persistent, but I will dispense with them for you so you can get on with your writing. The more deeply you engage your creative unconscious, the more you will diminish the power your demon fears have over you. It's all a matter of focusing your attention to what you most love doing, which is writing. So, just write!"

"I had a thought as I was walking up the stairs with Penny's coffee, and I'd like to run it by you; a thought about how independent of mind I seem to be now. I noticed this while talking with Sharon, a woman who just read my twin soul books. She cried when she read *Death, the Final Frontier* because it brought resolution to her spiritual quest and that gave me so much satisfaction that I had to invite her over for another talk, and during our second talk I couldn't get over how much I have grown in my gnostic understanding of the secret way. What do you think, Padre; have I come as far as I think I have, or am I being too generous with myself?"

"Not generous enough, I would say. Yes, you have come a long way in your gnostic understanding, and it shows in your conversations, especially when you let your inner self speak for you. This is happening more and more, and you will one day be free to speak as freely as you have dreamt of speaking. Your inner self won't be censored by your mind. It will happen soon enough, but do not expect a dramatic change in your personality. It will be gradual for you, but those who do not know you so well will see how different you are from everyone. You did experience it with Barbara as you talked about your books and the secret way, but you will express your independence of mind much more often in your everyday conversations."

"Padre, I don't want to talk just for the sake of talking with you; I want to be meaningful in our conversations, and for this I have to have something to say. So, if you don't mind, let's bring this talk to closure for the day, and I'll get back to you whenever."

"You're in a quandary as to what to get into next, but finish editing your sequel to the Hemingway book and take it from there. I'm here whenever you need me."

Thank you, Until again...

24. Talk Time

"I feel like the life is being sucked out of me, illegitimately, like a phantom vampire of my own making, a false demon born of my apprehensions, and this is getting very fatiguing and I don't know what to do about it. Any suggestions, Padre?"

"How about doing something? You thought you might want to finish staining your back deck. That would take your mind off your phantom demon."

"But it wouldn't solve my problem, would it?"

"On the contrary, doing is the answer to your problem. The more you do, the less your phantom demons will have power over you; and you're correct to call them phantom demons."

"But are they really phantom demons?"

"Yes, most of them are. You do have some real demons which you created out of your repressed guilt, but that's not what's bothering you. Your phantom demons are the result of shirking your duties. The more you shirk your duties, the more your phantom demons will bother you. As I said, doing is your answer. You have to break the habit of feeding your phantom demons with more worry. You worry for nothing, my friend. I assure you, everything is fine."

"With the triplex?"

"As I said, everything will be fine. Everything will be in place by the end of the week and that phantom demon will evaporate into the great void where it came from."

"Do you think then we can begin the sequel to *Healing with Padre Pio?*"

"That's what I'm waiting for."

25. What Now Brown Cow?

"Good morning, Padre. I'm opening up a dialogue this morning because I feel out of sorts—again, and again, and again. Sounds like that Shakespearean line, "out, out brief candle! Life's but a walking shadow, a poor player /That struts and frets his hour upon the stage /And then is heard no more." That's how I feel. But I'm going to make my coffee, and then we can have a little chat on this, my melancholy mood…"

"Good morning, my friend. I've been waiting for you."

"You do know that this is going to be a serious talk. I just read a poem while waiting for my first cup of coffee, which I spiked with a good dose of brandy (I need it this morning), from an article in this month's *Harper's Magazine,* "American Expansion, The innovations of A. R. Ammons," by Helen Vendler (I have her book on Emily Dickinson which I'm currently reading), and she quotes a poem by Ammons that I have to quote here because it speaks to the spiritual musing that I'm currently working on, "The Unlived Life" (I may change the title to "The Land of Lost Content") and the state of consciousness that I'm in this morning—

Easter Morning

I have a life that did not become,
that turned aside and stopped,
astonished:
I hold it in me like a pregnancy or
on my lap as a child
not to grow or grow old but dwell on

it is to his grave I most
frequently return and return
to ask what is wrong, what was
wrong, to see it all by

the light of a different necessity
but the grave will not heal
and the child,
stirring, must share my grave
with me, an old man having
gotten by on what was left.

"What a telling poem. Yes, it does speak to how you feel. But tell me, anyway."

"Of course, the merciful law of divine synchronicity was at work this morning, because for me to read that article while waiting for the coffee had to be divinely orchestrated. It was exactly what I needed to put this whole melancholy mood of mine into perspective. But why this melancholy mood, anyway? I woke up feeling this way, like I had no reason to go on with my life, like there was absolutely no point to anything because it all fell short of being relevant to the big scheme of things. In a word, Padre; I felt insignificant this morning."

"Not a nice place to be. But why is that? Isn't that because you failed to follow up on what you promised Penny? That you were going to look into getting some paint so you could start painting the house? How do you think Penny feels?"

"It's more than that. This speaks to my whole life. You told me that I came back to live my same life over again so that I could achieve a different outcome; well, here I am, twenty-some books later (with a few more to come) and, where am I? Did I achieve a different outcome?"

"Yes. You realized your true self. In your first lifetime, you failed. You died unresolved. You came back to your same life because you had a golden opportunity to live it again, but differently; and you did, with the result that you found your lost soul. What more could one ask of one's life?"

"Then why does Ammon's poem "Easter Morning" speak to me? Why do I feel like I never really lived the life I could have lived, even if I did find my lost soul?"

"No life will ever be perfect, regardless how many times one lives it. You have regrets, and these regrets are now affecting you. You are approaching the end of your life, and in this realization

(though you fail to acknowledge it) you feel you could have done better for yourself and your loved one, which you could have. But everything considered, you did well for yourself and Penny. You gave her a life that she would never have had. You gave her love. You would have liked to given her more, but life demanded more of you than your love for her, and you were obligated to life; and you fulfilled your obligation to life. Now try to fulfill your obligation to your loved one. You still have time. Give her the love she needs. Satisfy her demands of you."

"Is this my 'pregnancy,' to quote the poem above? Am I pregnant with unrealized responsibilities? Is that what's bothering me?"

"Yes, and much more. You still have a number of books that are begging to be finished and published, and not until you do will you feel justified in living your life over again. You did find your lost soul, but you have to tell your story to its conclusion; and to do that you have to get the books that are in you written. That's the only way you can satisfy your conscience."

"Like the book I started but didn't get into like I should have, *My Dearest Penny Lynn*?"

"Yes. You owe it to your love. You have to write this book of letters. It will satisfy you like no other book you have written. Please, do your best to complete this book. You will know when it is completed. Trust me, my friend; this book will revitalize you, and your relationship."

"Okay, but I need help. I need encouragement. I need the energy to do it. Can you help me realize this need to do right by Penny?"

"Of course, I will help you. This is why I'm here. We made a pact to help each other in our mutual goal of bringing to light the greater truth of the secret way, and not to give you a big head but you have done much more than I had expected. You exceeded everyone's expectations."

"By everyone, you mean?"

"We are not alone in our endeavor. We are a group of souls dedicated to making the secret teaching of the way of life known to the world. Your writing has done more to do this than any writer in the

world, believe it or not. This is why it's important for you to complete your life by writing all the books that your muse asks of you."

"My muse is unforgiving!"

"That's a good thing, believe it or not. Many writers would love to be in your shoes. You have a muse that won't give up on you. Just keep on writing as the inspiration comes to you. That's how you can overcome this mood of melancholy. And do Penny proud by satisfying her simple requests to get her house in order, will you please?"

"Can you give me an extra boost of energy for this, please?"

"Done!"

"Okay. I think I can get back to my spiritual musing now. I think that poem I read this morning was meant for this musing."

"It was. Good luck. We'll talk again..."

26. "You're a Fraud!"

Inspired by a dream experience

Thursday, August 17, 2017

"Padre, I had a dream the other night that I have to share with you. I was laying on my bed just now trying to rest (I slept poorly last night, as I often do), but the thought for a spiritual musing came to me and I had to get up to jot it down, and then I lay down to rest again and I was compelled to get up and share my dream with you; no doubt, because I want to hear what you have to say about it. Will you give me your interpretation of my dream?"

"It needs no interpretation, but we can discuss it if you wish. And good morning to you, if I may offer my greetings."

"You certainly can, and I apologize for my impropriety. Incidentally, I was inspired this morning to dip into Glenda Green's book *Love Without End, Jesus Speaks,* which you recommended when I was having my spiritual healing sessions that inspired my novel *Healing with Padre Pio,* and it felt good re-reading the book; it picked up my spirits, which was probably why I was inspired with the idea for a spiritual musing on doing, which is something that you always keep telling me to do to get myself out of my funks, and the title that came to me for this spiritual musing was: 'The Magical Healing Properties of Doing.' What do you think?"

"Excellent topic. Explore it when you have more energy. This musing requires your best energies, so don't take it on unless you are really up to it. Now, about your dream?"

"In my dream, I was in a large room with about three or four hundred followers of the New Age spiritual teaching of the Light and Sound of God that Penny and I dropped out of two or three years ago, and we were listening to the Spiritual Leader of this teaching speaking; but what he was saying about me was false. He was telling the audience that I was promoting this New Age teaching of the Light and Sound of God (I refuse to mention its public domain name) through my writing, thereby appropriating me into this teaching the way the founder of this teaching appropriated (purloined, is more like it) ancient spiritual teachings to create a new teaching for the modern world and calling it the most ancient of spiritual teachings, also creating Spiritual Masters out of thin air to advance this teaching, and appropriating Spiritual Masters from other ancient spiritual traditions like St. Paul and Milarepa and installing them into the lineage of this New Age spiritual teaching of the Light and Sound of God; and I stood up and the Spiritual Leader saw me, and our eyes locked and he flinched because he had been found out. That's when I shouted: *'You're a Fraud!'* And I walked out of the room, and a number of other people got up and walked out also. And outside, someone came up to me and asked me something, and I told him that I was once a High Initiate of this teaching and went through my wallet to show him my HI (High Initiate) card, but couldn't find it. What do you think of the dream, Padre? Was it an inner experience, or symbolic?"

"Both. You have built up the momentum through your writing to enter the ethers with your integrity, and you now pose a serious threat to this teaching. It was a long time coming."

"Is he a fraud like I said he is?"

"You didn't have to ask me that, but I will answer all the same. Yes, he is a fraud. He didn't start out that way. Like you, he was totally sincere and accepted upon faith alone the sincerity of the teaching; but he got caught up in the vortex of the teaching and didn't have the courage to walk away from it like you did. It was a necessary dream which confirms your position with this teaching. You are now free to move on without any attachment whatsoever."

"Are we ever going to get together for a sequel to *Healing with Padre Pio* so we can discuss this further?"

"Yes."

"Good; I'm looking forward to it. I started painting the house the other day and am planning to get back to it today, that's why I was resting; but I got called by my muse!"

"I know. Go and rest and get back to your painting. Get some momentum going and you will paint the whole house before you know it. I will boost your energy."

"Thank you, Padre."

"You're welcome…"

71

27. I Feel Like I'm Out at Sea, Floundering

Saturday, August 26, 2017

"Good morning, Padre. I wasn't going to open up a chat-line with you this morning, but I felt a need to talk with you after I posted my musing "Being the Tao" and then looking up some books on Carl Jung and his psychology when I got swamped by a feeling of smallness, like I was out at sea again and floundering; well, not quite floundering like I did when I was studying philosophy at university because I've come a long way since, but floundering in a different kind of way, like I'm tired of all the seeking and questing and wondering that one has to do to get to where he is meant to be, and since I am already where I am meant to be I feel a little perplexed in my floundering; can you make any sense of this feeling?"

"Good morning, my friend. It's good to have you back!"

"What do you mean by that?"

"'You're back on track to the purpose of your life, which is to write about your own life experiences and not worry about others, as such. Your own life is the way, and because it has brought you to where you were meant to be, what does it matter how others get there? Not that I suggest you don't care about how others get to where they are meant to be, but by telling your story—as it happens to you on a daily basis—you reveal the mysteries of the way, just as you did in your latest spiritual musing 'Being the Tao.' That's you in action, being yourself; and in being yourself, you reveal the mysteries of the way. That's what I mean by welcoming you back."

"Wonderful, but that doesn't change how I feel. I still feel like I'm floundering, and I don't particularly care for this feeling. It makes me feel small. Like there's so much more I need to know. I don't feel false in my own gnostic knowledge, but I feel like I need to grow, and I don't quite know how to do that other than through more reading; but looking up those books I did this morning, I said to myself—what the hell for? I'm where they are striving to get to, so why should I worry about getting to know their story, their journey of self-discovery. But I also relish in this knowledge, because I've always been interested in another person's journey. Do you see my quandary, as foolish as it may appear?"

*"It's perfectly natural. Just because you have become what you were meant to be doesn't mean you can't be curious about the journey of self-discovery as it is expressed by the rest of world, especially the literary world. You have the advantage of knowing the way, so you can see it in someone else's journey of self-discovery. That's what makes your story fascinating. You have become your own Tao, to use your expression in your last spiritual musing; and being your own Tao, you have the gnostic wisdom of the way to appreciate the process of becoming as it is expressed by other seekers. That's why you love reading. Yes, I can see you feeling overwhelmed by another person's knowledge, especially if they are exceptionally brilliant like professor Harold Bloom; but that's only natural. Trust yourself. Trust your own experiences. Trust your own knowledge. Your knowledge is gnostic. It is who you are, because you lived what you believed. That's what makes you different. It's in the living of one's beliefs that one gains gnostic knowledge. That's what makes it gnostic. It becomes who you are, and you **are** your knowledge. It isn't just data in your mind. Write about what you are, not what you know as they say in creative writing classes. You **are** what you know, and your life is your story."*

"I'm beginning to feel a little better, but not quite enough to get on with my day. I have to feel more resolved in my situation. How can I go about doing that?"

"As always, by doing. Doing will give you the energy you need to stand above your situation. Didn't Penny say to you yesterday that you looked young, like you had the look of someone who got a monkey off his back? Doing will get all the monkeys off your back, and you still have a few; so just do, live your life and do. Get those monkeys off your back. That's how you will feel resolved."

"I know. And I did feel resolved yesterday after I finished painting the washroom. It felt good to get that monkey off my back. I will finish it completely before I paint my writing den, and then I will move on to another room. I told Penny I will get the whole house painted even if it kills me, and it might because my work-capacity just isn't there because of my heart condition; but at least the house will be more marketable if I go. That's what I said to Penny, and even though I was joking it felt good to say it. I do have a few more books to write, so I don't think I will go just yet. Besides, we have to get our sequel to *Healing with Padre Pio* written."

"We do, and we will. Just do what you feel you have to do and all will be well; I promise you, my friend. Now get on with your day. We'll talk again soon."

"We will..."

28. What's Wrong with this Picture?

Sunday, August 27, 2017

"One day, just one day I'd like to have no apprehension on my mind; just one day, Padre. Gosh, this makes me feel foolish. How many times did you sit in the confessional booth listening to all the moaning and whining and crying and grieving? One would think you'd be free of all that now, and here I am moaning and groaning like some child who wants the world to go its way. What's wrong with this picture?"

"You're out of focus. You have to get your focus back, and you can do that by consolidating your energies; and you can consolidate your energies by writing. Writing always brings you into correct focus, because writing taps into your creative principle; and your creative principle knows what's best for you, because your creative principle is your higher self."

"Maybe this is why I'm chatting with you now. Maybe this is how I can get myself back into focus. After all, you are my creative principle—*n'est ce pas?*"

"Correct. So, what would you like to chat about?"

"Why hasn't anyone of consequence picked up one of my books and explored it? I'm thinking of my synchronicity book at the moment. I watched a video last night, for the second or third time, on synchronicity—specialists in their field, physics and psychology—and they skirt around the edges of this subject, like dogs sniffing a piece of meat to see if its good to eat. What the hell is going on out there, Padre?"

"You have every right to be frustrated. Your perspective on synchronicity touches upon the sacred mystery of the way, and they are not ready yet for this realization; but you will be seen to be ahead of your time, in good time."

"Yeah, right! You can't deflect with your humor, regardless how correct you are; please tell me, Padre, what the hell is going on out there? Why am I not being acknowledged?"

"The answer is that life is an individual journey. You will be found by those who need your insights into the sacred knowledge of the way. I assure you."

"Just not in my lifetime, right?"

"Yes, in your lifetime. Just keep writing. It will come."

"I'm losing steam, Padre. I don't know if I can step into that stream again. I feel like I'm beginning to fade. I know I need to focus, but I feel like I'm fading."

"Your well needs to be replenished. Just let life happen. Don't worry. I promise, all of your life concerns are taken care of. Don't worry about your trip up north. All is well. You will have a wonderful time. You will come back replenished. You will have one of the most productive winters of your life. You will write one of your best books."

"And what book will that be?"

"Give it to your muse. You will surprise yourself."

"I have a feeling that I will complete and get *The Armchair Guru* out, complete my poetry book *A Bouquet of Wild Flowers*, and possibly my book of short stories, and then I will embark upon a personal narrative, perhaps *An Elephant in the Room*. How close am I?"

"You can be right on if you want it to be. But that's deflecting. I can tell you that you will embark upon a new story, and it will preoccupy you all winter. It will be so preoccupying that you will feel creatively sated like no other time in your life, because this story will tell the whole truth about your journey to wholeness and completeness. You are ready to write this story."

"I know I am, but will I ever get it started?"

"Yes. This winter."

"I have the strongest feeling it will be my story based upon the funeral experience of my friend Alice. My working title is 'An Elephant in the Room.' Is that it?"

"If you want it to be."

"I do. But can I make it happen?"

"Yes."

"I always need an inspiration to embark upon a new book. Will I get one?"

A Sign of Things to Come

"You have the inspiration. You just need to focus your attention. When the time is right, it will happen; and that will be this coming winter. I know you are tired of hearing it, but I promise it will happen. And you can check that I told you so when it does happen."

"I really don't have a choice, do I? I just have to let my life unfold."

"Yes. Now get on with your day, and be blessed in your unfolding. I am always with you, and I promise to keep you safe. My love for you and your loved one."

"Thank you…"

29. You Did Promise to Keep Me Safe

Monday, August 28, 2017

"I don't really want to talk with you this morning, Padre; but I have to. I got into a vehicle accident yesterday and I remember what you said to me as we brought our chat to closure. *'I am always with you, and I promise to keep you safe,'* you said; and, well, I did not get hurt, and neither did Penny, but I feel absolutely foolish for my stupidity. That's what I have to talk about with you today—the Trickster, my idiot self if you will. Are you willing to discuss this with me? I can understand if you don't want to, but I have to explore this curious accident that has thrown a little confusion into our life. It was like I went through a fog yesterday, and I want to know why; or, rather, I want to know if I'm correct in my reasoning—that I taunted the Trickster with the spiritual musing that I posted the day before, 'Being the Tao.'"

"The short answer is a resounding YES. The long answer requires some explanation. You have been building up to this little awakening for some time now. Fortunately, you weren't hurt, and neither was your loved one; but you did invite the Trickster energy into your life, and that's what I'd like to talk about with you today. You're right in your insight, the Trickster is the shadow side of your personality, and it exists as the transformer of one's life in every person's personality because it is the negative aspect of your nature that needs transformation, and it is to its nature to seek transformation because it has to become what one is meant to be, whole and completely oneself. The Trickster has to come out when no other avenue is open to you to realize the transformation of your shadow self, and it will come out spontaneously just as it did yesterday when you switched lanes without looking to see if there was a vehicle behind you. It was, as you said, stupid, and it was entirely your fault; but that's what the Trickster does. It is, as you so rightly believe, the 'idiot self' of the personality; but it is not idiotic, as such.

A Sign of Things to Come

It is brilliant in its idiocy because it seeks transformation, and the outcome of the experience is more growth and understanding. Didn't I tell you that life is all about growth and understanding. Well, you were in need of more growth and understanding, and there you have it—you brought it upon yourself through the unconscious activation of your idiot self. Any comment so far?

"None. I'm sorry for the inconvenience this is causing Penny; but it's my lesson, is it not?"

"It is your lesson insomuch that you brought it on yourself, but out of this Penny will grow in understanding also. It is good for both of you, but especially you. You do need to take more care of your life, my friend. You need to get a good night's sleep. If you would have had a good night's sleep you would not have ended up in the accident yesterday. You weren't alert enough to see what you were doing. The morale of this experience is to be mindful, and mindfulness is always enhanced by a good night's sleep. You have to work on that."

"I know. Alright, now the vanity issue. Did my spiritual musing yesterday stir up the shadow in me? Is that why the Trickster came out to play havoc with my life, and Penny's life? I can't help but feel that my deep sense of 'gnostic pride,' if I may call it that, stirred up the shadow forces of my life which manifested into the Archetypal Trickster. Am I right or wrong?"

"Absolutely right. You did stir up your shadow forces with your gnostic pride, and you were brought down a peg or two. That was the purpose of the experience. As you like to say, 'life is a journey through vanity to humility.'"

"So, I have a new spiritual musing to write up. My working title is 'The Trickster.' I just wanted to run this by you first. I don't know if I can write it this week, but I want to post next Saturday on the heels of my musing 'Being the Tao.' It's ironic, don't you think?"

"Yes, it is. But don't be concerned, everything will unfold gracefully. Your lessons have been learned, your gnostic pride has been tempered, and all will be well for a long while, unless you stir up the shadow forces again and call up the Archetypal Trickster."

"Maybe that's what I should call my new spiritual musing, 'The Archetypal Trickster.' It seems to be more accurate."

"It is. I prefer it. But it's up to you, of course."

"Okay, Padre; now we have to go through all the humbling, lesson-learning hassle of dealing with our insurance and getting our car repaired. The whole right door was smashed in, including the mirror, and the front hood panel as well. We'll see how that goes. This means that Penny and I won't be making our trip up north. How's that going to turn out?"

"Very well, I promise you. Now take a break, collect yourself, and do a little painting and get your two washrooms completed. It will please Penny."

"I know. Thank you, Padre."

"You're welcome, my friend..."

30. Deep Talk, Please?

Tuesday, August 30, 2017

"Good morning, Padre. I'd like to talk deep today, if you don't mind. I'd like to talk about the paradigm shift that's coming, if it isn't already here, the paradigm shift from a material-based perspective on life to a consciousness-centered perspective, if I'm on the right track that is. Can you enlighten me on this?"

"This shift has been happening for the past few years now, since 2012 when the agencies of God's creation came to Planet Earth's assistance. A call went out for all the souls that would help the world make this shift in consciousness, and souls from higher frequencies came to the world's aid to help raise the planet's vibrations. This is happening now."

"I just read a report that the IQ of the world's population is dropping. Is the world getting more stupid? What's going on?"

"The world is growing in a way that cannot be measured. Soul is going through a deep-cleansing. It needs to be cleansed so the world's vibrations can be raised. The mental state is in a state of confusion; that's why the world's IQ is dropping. It won't last. Once the world's new frequency sets in, the IQ of the world will go up."

"Where do I fit in in all of this? Is my writing reflecting this change of frequency?"

"Yes, much more than you realize."

"I get the feeling that all I need to do is listen to my muse."

"Your muse is in tune with the higher frequencies of life. Yes, by all means give your writing to your muse, with conscious direction, just as you are doing."

"Need I do more reading on the subject? Like Penny Peirce's book, *Leap of Perception* which I just took off my shelf yesterday to re-read?"

"It wouldn't hurt to remind yourself of what you already know, to bring it to your conscious mind so you can familiarize yourself with the terminology; but essentially, the creative process is

the connection to the higher frequencies. Just write. That's your connection."

"Was my vehicle accident a shift in frequencies?"

"You needed to be reminded of your state of consciousness. You needed a humbling experienced because of your gnostic conceit. You got it, now learn from it and get on with your life."

"I gave a copy of my poetry book *Not My Circus, Not My Monkeys* to my neighbors yesterday when they were out walking their dogs. I hope I didn't jar their paradigm."

"They need the jarring. Your book will do them more good than you can imagine. They need to shift their priorities from the good life to the noble life, a life of sharing and giving; your book will help them make the shift. Trust the process, my friend."

"I hope this doesn't scare them. I can be a bit much for people."

"You can be, and are for most people; but not in this case. They know how far advanced you are in your thinking, and they respect you enough to check you out."

"What about that shadow-afflicted neighbor across the street? Is he destined to be my irritation? I'm glad Penny saw his measure the other day. He revealed his shadow self and put Penny off. What to do?"

"Nothing. His life is his life. Let the law of life work it out. Just live your life. You are too much for his ego and he's terrified of you, resentful of you, and wants to pull you down to his level; but he knows he can't, and it frustrates him. You threaten his self-image."

"Back to this paradigm shift. Will it ever happen in my lifetime? I don't think it will, but I think I'm helping the shift with my writing."

"You are. Just let the process work itself out. You are doing your part, and there's nothing more you can do. Not at this time in your life. Just write and trust the process."

"You've used this expression 'trust the process' several times now. Are you trying to tell me something I'm not getting?"

"It all comes back to you. You have to trust yourself and your writing. You have made the connection with your superior insight, what more can you do; so, just trust the process."

"And Bob's your uncle, as the English like to say."

A Sign of Things to Come

"Yes. It is what it is."

"I got a nudge to write something new, like I said the other day, maybe my story 'The Elephant in the Room,' but I'm not quite smitten yet. Will I get smitten by my muse, because that's the only way I'll ever commit to writing it?"

"This book will happen when it happens. You will know when. I can tell you now that it will not be what you expect. It will be more than what you expect. It will be your story of your growth through the teaching that you outgrew and left. It will be a great story, my friend."

"I want it to be my most literary story."

"It will be."

"I got the feeling just now that it will be over four hundred pages."

"Very close. It will be a big novel."

"Will I get it first-drafted this coming winter?"

"Perhaps."

"And my other work?"

"In conjunction with your other work."

"About my dream last night. Should I be worried? My dream was too personal to disclose."

"It was a compensatory dream, working out your anxieties. Nothing to worry about."

"Do you have anything you would like to say to me?"

"I believe in you. Just write and make me proud."

"Thank you…"

31. Interrupted Chat

Thursday, August 31, 2017

"Good morning, Padre. I feel a presentment of winter writing. It came to me while I was reading *Speaking from the Heart,* subtitled *Ethics, Reincarnation & What It Means to Be Human*, by Joan Grant, the novelist gifted with what she called "far memory," but just as I started this morning's chat I got a phone call from our friend Sharon, and she's going to drop over for a visit; so, if you don't mind, I'll pick this up later."

"Not at all. Enjoy your visit with your friend. She's a very special lady who has taken to your writing. As you said, she is the forerunner of the kind of people who will flock to your writing once the call goes out into the ethers by her compassion for your teachings. Wait and see how her appreciation for your writing will cause a ripple in the ethers. So, by all means, enjoy your visit and we'll talk again whenever you're ready."

"Thank you for understanding. Until then…"

"I'm back. Sorry for the delay, but after Sharon's visit yesterday I wasn't up to resuming our talk. She brought over some sweet yellow corn and yellow beans, and we sat on my front deck and sipped herbal tea and talked until Penny came home from work, and then we had a glass of wine and talked some more. It was a wonderful conversation, because Sharon pulls out of me what she needs to hear, which always comes as a surprise to me, like what I said about one of my neighbors who is going to model for one of my characters in my novel-to-be, *We May Be Tiny, But We're Not Small*; I said, "He's the way he is because he is his shadow." By this I meant that his shadow has taken over his personality and he can't help being as miserable as he is, because it's his nature to be that way. What do you say about that, Padre?"

"You gained a valuable insight into your neighbor as you talked with your friend Sharon, and it will make for a rich and

complex character in your novel. This novel will be the one you will tell the story that needs to be told in the literary genre that you crave to write. Do not worry about when it will be written, you may get to it this winter or you may not (you will be writing your funeral service story first), but when you write it you will get so involved that you will feel like the creative writer you always dreamt of being. It was a nice visit. Sharon loved it."

"What do you say about my insight of the shadow taking over my neighbor's personality? Is his ego so permeated by his shadow that he is his shadow 24/7?"

"Yes. This is what makes him so miserable. This is the core of his personality which you will reveal in your novel. You have enough anecdotal material to bring him to life in your story, as you do with your other characters; but keep taking notes. It's the anecdotes that will give your story the flesh and bones of a good story."

"I have to tell you that I posted a new spiritual musing on my blog this morning. It's called 'The Old Trickster,' and it has to do with the trickster aspect of our shadow personality. I have no idea how it will be received. What do you think of it?"

"A very penetrating insight into the nature of man's unconscious personality. It will be one to be remembered. One of your very best musings."

"Sometimes I get the feeling that these musings are all I am meant to write, but I know that's not true because when I am called to write another book I have no choice but to write it or suffer the consequences of feeling unfulfilled; so, when am I going to be called to write another book? Can you tell me? This winter, as I felt yesterday?"

"Yes. Once you get your house almost painted you will be called. You will continue to paint your house as you write your new novel, but you will be called."

"Do I suspect my book of short stories will be finished, my book *Sparkles in the Mist*?"

"Yes. It will be your warm-up book for your new novel."

"Today is the first day of the long weekend, Labour Day Weekend, and I'd like to take Penny somewhere. She said we may be going out tomorrow because the traffic won't be as heavy, and we may go sight-seeing, maybe to Meaford or Orillia or the Muskoka area, we don't know; but I think we're going somewhere. We got a call from the body shop and they're waiting for the parts for the car, then he will call us and we can book our car for repairs. We're very happy with the way our insurance handled the whole thing. It was very smooth. I hope it ends that way."

"It will. You learned your lesson, which many of your readers will appreciate."

"The journey through vanity to humility never ends, does it?"

"Not while you still have an ego."

"Which we cannot ever not have while still in our body, isn't that so?"

"Correct, my friend. But you have come a long way in your realization. Your writing will be invaluable when your readers get to see the depths of your insights."

"I read Joan Grant's book *Speaking from the Heart* yesterday, and although I enjoyed reading it (I skim-read a lot of it), it proved no less validating; but it left me with the impression that I have moved on from this kind of literature because I no longer need confirmation for this kind of life-experience. My own life is proof enough for me."

"That's what I keep trying to tell you."

"Well, I'm re-reading my own book *The Merciful Law of Divine Synchronicity* again, and I just love it. I shared this with Sharon the other day and she thought it was precious. She was brought to tears again just thinking about how they moved her to tears when she read both this book and its twin soul, *Death, the Final Frontier*. I do hope these books go viral!"

"Give them a chance."

"Okay, Padre; thank you for chatting with me."

"You're welcome…"

32. A Spiritual Musing For My Russian Readers

Tuesday, September 5, 2017

"Good morning, Padre. I just want to tell you that I wrote a new spiritual musing called "The Tremor of Eternity," and I posted it on my blog yesterday. I wrote this for my Russian readers. Actually, this thought came later; I wrote it because the idea floated around in my head (actually, it feels like it floated around and above my head; somewhere in my energy field), and I had to get it out, which I did, and then the thought came to me to post it in honor of my Russian readers, because I do get a lot of Russian readers for my spiritual musings blog. But when Penny and I were talking yesterday, I made an interesting discovery. It just came to me that the Russian people are up against a great mystery: where does their suffering take them? What lies on the other side of existential anguish? That's why I think I get so many Russians reading my blog, because they are pulled into the mystery that I have solved. What do you think?"

"You are absolutely correct. They need to know why they have to endure the suffering that they do. What purpose does it serve? Your spiritual musings intrigue your Russian readers, and this is only the beginning. Your new post will excite their imagination, and it will go viral in Russian. Wait and see."

"I don't feel very creative today. I plan to begin painting my writing room today, which I've been putting off, but this morning I feel a little out of sorts. I think it was my sleep. I did not sleep very well, and my dreams didn't help any. I'm not where I want to be."

"And where would you like to be?"

"Free of anxiety. Free of a lot of things. Free of life, really."

"I know the feeling well, my friend. But you too must serve your time. This is what you contracted to do, and do it you will. You have a few more books to write yet, and many more to finish and publish; so just get on with your life and don't worry about it."

"I like that attitude. I only wish I could adopt it."

"You will, and you do practically every day. Focus your attention. That's where to start. If you don't feel like chatting any more, read and focus your attention."

"Question. Did my book of poetry affect my neighbors? I gave them my book *Not My Circus, Not My Monkeys,* and I feel that it affected them. I feel they are being thoughtful about life now. That they are taking stock of their life, if you will."

"Your book has made them rethink their life. They are not so smug in their material accomplishments now. Your book has given them pause to reflect upon their life. You did them a great service, and they don't know how to deal with it yet."

"About my Russian readers. How will my new musing affect them?"

"They are respectful of your understanding. They will honor you by reading you."

"And my English readers?"

"You continue to puzzle them."

"I feel that I understand the paradigm shift that's taking place, and I will probably write a spiritual musing on it when I'm called to do so. I feel the call will be coming soon. I don't know when, but I can feel the idea formulating somewhere in my energy field."

"The seed has been planted, and it will sprout in a month or two. You will write it."

"But am I correct in my insight that the paradigm shift is one of consciousness? From the material-centered to consciousness-centered?"

"Fundamentally, yes. It will be gradual, but the shift has started. Man can no longer deny the continuity of life. This is the shift that's taking place, a shift from doubt to certainty."

"Because science deems it? Physics is proving the continuity of life, isn't it?"

"Quantum physics, yes."

"Is this why the demons (false beliefs) are running scared?"

"That's a good way of putting it. Yes, they are running scared. This is why there is such turmoil in society. The frequency is changing, and the demons can't bear it."

A Sign of Things to Come

"I started a work called 'My Pythagorean Project,' but it's not going anywhere. I can't seem to get into it. The initial idea excited me, but I can't seem to be pulled into it."

"You're not ready for that project yet, but it is a good idea. It will be an exercise in creative exploration, and you will learn a lot about yourself from that past lifetime."

"Any advice on how to jump into this project? How can I awaken my deep memory?"

"The same way you chat with me."

"Only with Pythagoras?"

"Yes. And eventually, with your other lifetime. You can explore this another time. For now, focus on painting your house and your stories. You have to write your book Sparkles in the Mist. *It is crying to be published. Work on it, please."*

"I'll try…"

33. Not Feeling Creative

Monday, September 11, 2017

"Good morning, Padre. Need to talk. Not feeling creative. Wanted to work on my spiritual musing, but I don't have it in me. Am anxious again. Don't know why, it should be normal by now; but it's not. Got a call yesterday from one of our tenants. She has no hot water. Maybe the pilot light on the water tank went out. The water tank is also part of the water-heating system for the apartment. Hope that's all it is. Will call this morning for the tradesman to go. Why did it have to happen? Things were going so well. We're going to get our car fixed from my stupid accident. I don't know if I told you about my accident, but if I didn't I wrote a musing on it. I just need to talk, Padre. I need to go into a corner and cry, and cry. That's how I feel. And yet, the people in Florida are in a mess from Hurricane Irma. Why do I worry over such little things? I think it's more than that. I think I'm worrying about my writing life. I think I want out of this whole damn thing called life. What can I do but wait?"

"You can wait. You can hide in a corner and cry. You can do any number of things. Why don't you just perk up and get your jobs done? Call your heating man, it isn't anything serious. Work on you room today. Read, write, and get on with your life. It's all good, my friend."

"I'm going downstairs to make coffee. Back in a bit…"

"I'm back. Read the rest of my Virginia Woolf biography and didn't feel anything. Am glad I read it because it gave me an insight into her life that I didn't recognize, her radical spirit, her courage, but also her selfishness which I believe was the cause of her mental illness. She was too self-centered, but she was a breakaway writer who set the stage for the modern movement with her iconoclastic take on life. She inspired many women. Anyway, I don't know what else I can say but that I don't have it in me to write today. I feel like it's all a waste for some reason. Why this feeling of inadequacy?"

A Sign of Things to Come

"It happens. Life is cyclical. You have your ups and downs. You are in a down cycle. It's not too bad, though. You have no thoughts of suicide like Virginia Woolf. She was fighting her down cycle most of her life. You did learn a lot from her life. It will show in your writing, as it did in your spiritual musing "The Satisfaction of Doing and the Mystery of Soul-Making.' It gave you perspective. Just write whatever comes to your mind."

"Am I escaping myself with my writing, or am I confronting myself?"

"Neither. You are a servant of your muse."

"Where is my muse today?"

"Standing right behind you. Over your right shoulder. Smiling."

"Why would my muse be smiling?"

"Because life is good. You are well into the goodness of your life and you are about to write the most significant book you will ever write. It is the story of the quest, but told in the story of your life. I won't go into detail, but it isn't that far off. Trust me. You are here now, where you are meant to be. You do have a room of your own, and your room is your sanctuary. It is where you wrote and worked out the mystery of becoming. You will write and write and write."

"Do I have to keep contending with these pesky little worries, like our triplex?"

"Not for much longer. You will be free of them within a short time. You will have all the worry-free time to write and write and write."

"I'll probably have serious health issues by then."

"No. You will not. You will write and write and write."

"Why do you keep saying that?"

"To impress upon you what you are. What you have become. What you have worked so hard to realize. You will write and write and write."

"I think my musing 'My Bonus Room' that I started the other day is going to go deep into my personal history. I think this musing may be an entry into something deeper."

"It will be. It will open the door to your novel "We May Be Tiny, But We're Not Small.'"

"Tell me, Padre; has my life become a joke?"

"Why do you ask?"

"Because that's how I feel. I've spent my life figuring out why I did what I did that night so many years ago, which compelled me to go on my quest for my true self, and I did find my true self; but now I wonder, what was all the fuss about? Life is like that for everybody, and everybody has to find their own way out of the shadow side of their life; so now I wonder, what have I contributed to the process? No one cares. Everyone has their own life to live, and there's nothing I can say or write that will make a difference; or am I fooling myself?"

"You have made a difference in a lot of lives. Just keep writing, my friend. Your time is approaching. Your writing will find its niche in the marketplace. It isn't far off."

"Could I be so right in my perspective that I smile at all the others?"

"Your truth is your truth, and it serves you well. Other perspectives don't have the gnostic reality that yours has. That's the difference. And so, I say again, write and write and write."

"Padre, I'd like a graceful walk through the rest of our life. Penny and I deserve it. Can it possibly be? I pray that it will."

"It is already, my friend. Just keep doing what you're doing. You have put a lot of the pieces together, and only a few more to go before you see what you want to see."

"Okay. Thank you."

"You're welcome...."

34. A Sexual Metaphor for British Imperialism

Thursday, September 14. 2017

"Good morning, Padre. Don't know what I want to talk about this morning, but I do want to sit and chat with you just to get the juices flowing. Yesterday I frustrated myself putting together a bookcase, the third of a matching set that has been sitting for two or three years, and then showered and relaxed and watched several episodes of *Outlander* on Netflix, a television series based upon the novels by Diana Gabaldon, and I have to tell you, I was horrified by how the British treated the Scots, especially one Red Coat called Captain "Black Jack" and what he did to one Scotsman called Jamie Fraser. "Black Jack" seemed to embody the worst of the British, that deep perverse need to dominate and control and possess—a sexual metaphor, perhaps, for British imperialism. If so, the sexual metaphoric imagery was horrifying.

"And today I'm going to put up the new venetian blind and shift the books in my two shelves over into the bookcases by the walls I have painted, and then I can paint the remaining two walls of my Bonus Room. And then I can enjoy my writing room freshly painted and without clutter. But I have to tell you that this morning I went on Amazon and checked out some more of Updike's books, his collection of essays, book reviews, and whatnot, and once again I'm overwhelmed by his literary mastery. He frightens me, he's so prodigious in his output, and brilliant in his insights. What am I to do?"

"Nothing. As I said, John Updike had his genius and you have yours. Don't compare yourself to him or any other writer. If you like Updike, which apparently you do, then read him for the pleasure of his literary mastery. Enjoy him. Celebrate him. He earned it."

"I agree. He did earn it. He was industrious. Now, can I ask you about Diana Gabaldon's genius, because she obviously has a genius for historical novel writing. Did she draw upon past lives in the British Isles, Scotland and England?"

"Definitely. She could not have such easy affinity with her material if she didn't have past-life memories of her lives in the British Isles. She's very Celtic in her past-life history, and although she researches deeply for her novels, she taps into her subconscious memories and gives the reader a definite feel for authenticity."

"Would it be possible for me to do that?"

"Not for you, my friend. Your talent is for new thinking. Your work is for those who want to understand the meaning and purpose of life, not repeat it in historical fiction. Historical fiction is a talent for revealing the past to the present, which Diana Gabaldon does with extraordinary creative genius, but that's not your calling. You calling is for distilling the essential meaning of life experience and working it into a new way of conceptual thinking."

"This explanation would also apply to writers like John Updike who had a genius for writing about contemporary life as he saw and experienced it. He did it with enormous ease (which isn't to take away from his devotion to his craft) which has intimidated many writers, but that was his calling, and mine is different; is that what you are saying?"

"Precisely so."

"And my poetry, stories, novels, memoirs, and especially my spiritual musings are what I am called to write for the purpose of conceptualizing the inherent purpose and meaning of life?"

"I couldn't have put it better myself. Yes, that's what you are meant to do."

"I just wrote a poem this morning. I'm going to quote it and then ask what you think of it. I want to know if I'm on the right track with it:

THE GOOD NEWS

When a seeker of truth finds
what he's looking for,
what does he do? —

Tell the world the good news,
or go about his business like
nothing happened?

A Sign of Things to Come

He decides to tell the world,
not slant like Emily Dickinson,
but unveiled like Rumi, —

And the world calls him a fool!

"What do you think? Isn't this what a new way of thinking will do to me? Have the world call me a fool? Wasn't this why Emily Dickinson couched the secret way in her poetry?"

"It was, but look at the effect it has had on her readers? She was true to her calling and the world is still wondering about her hidden meaning. No, I don't think you are off the mark. The world puzzles over your writing, but not like it puzzles over Emily Dickinson because you reveal the secret in the open without apology. Your writing is a blend of Dickinson and Rumi, and it's your own particular genius. Just keep writing as you are. Let your muse guide you."

"And the poem?"

"It says what you want it to say."

"Presumptuous or not?"

"It is and it isn't. As I said, it's a blend of Dickinson and Rumi."

"Alright, Padre: I'm going to shut down and see if I can install the new venetian blind for my Bonus Room. And then I'm going to get the other two walls ready for painting. Thank you for the chat this morning."

"You're welcome…"

35. Losing My Fire

Saturday, September 16, 2017

"Good morning, Padre. Should I post my spiritual musing on my blog this morning? I'm feeling a little doubtful. Not doubtful, perhaps discouraged. I need some input."

"Your regular readers are looking forward to another spiritual musing. You did get a comment from one reader who said to keep writing, which is a sentiment felt by many of your readers even though they don't express it. Yes, by all means post it."

"Okay. Give me a moment or two."

"Certainly..."

"Okay, I'm back. I've posted my musing, 'Coincidences in the Blueberry Patch,' and then I posted it on Twitter and Facebook. I hope it attracts some readers."

"It will. Now get on with whatever you want to talk about and let your writing speak for itself. It will find its own readers. What do you have on your mind this morning?"

"I'm concerned that I may be losing my fire, if you know what I mean."

"I know exactly what you mean. And how do you propose to get your fire back?"

"Your suggestion has always been to focus. Focus and write and write and write. But if I am low in fire, how can I do that? That's my dilemma."

"You need a new writing project to get into. I suggest you complete your book of stories. Once you have worked your way through that you will have your fire back."

"You mean my book *Sparkles in the Mist*?"

"Yes. Work on it. Type up your last two stories and then edit and tighten them up and have Penny publish it. It will boost your morale."

"Can I ask you something, Padre?"

"By all means."

A Sign of Things to Come

"Do I really have any literary talent? I've been watching the *Outlander* series on Netflix and I was moved by the genius of the storyline. That's creative writing. Do I have talent for creative writing? That's my question."

"Yes, but not for historical novels. Your talent is more literary. You have your own genius for resolving the issues of the human condition. That's what literature does, it brings meaning and purpose to the reader through stories. Your writing is not for entertainment alone, it's for the edification of the soul. Your writing lifts up the human spirit. You were not called to write for entertainment alone; you were called to break through the barriers of the mind. That's your gift. That's your genius. That's what you are meant to do."

"A new way of thinking, you said to me in my novel *Healing with Padre Pio?*"

"And I will repeat it. You have provided a new way of thinking about life. You have found the way out of the human maze, and your calling is to let the world know. That's why I keep telling you to write."

"Is this why I'm called to write my spiritual musings?"

"Precisely so."

"Do you have any other suggestions on how to get my fire back?"

"You haven't lost it. But I can suggest on how you can build up the heat of your fire. You need to do some physical exercise for one. Walk more or cycle. Do that for at least ten to fifteen minutes a day. And drink five to seven glasses of water every day. That's the physical part. As for the rest, you must focus on one project and get it done, like your book of stories. And you may try something different. You may want to try sleeping without your radio. This will help immensely, because a good night's sleep replenishes your energies. And you know that your energy level is when your fire is the strongest. The more energy you have, the hotter your fire will be. That's a fact of life. Energy equals creativity. It's that simple. So, just work out how to build up more energy. You can use your Gurdjieffian work discipline—non-identifying, for example. Go to sanctuary, if you have to. That has always been a good way for you to collect yourself."

"You know what I'd really like to do?"

"What?"

"I'd like to read poetry every morning. I'd like to work my way through my word books and learn all the new words I can so I can conceptualize with more clarity. I really would love to work my way through three or four of my vocabulary-building books. Can you help me do that?"

"Done!"

"Just like that?"

"Yes."

"If I may ask, how have you helped me?"

"By planting the seed in your unconscious. You will be inspired by your own unconscious need to work your way through three or four vocabulary books. That's how I work."

"You've planted the seed, then?"

"Yes."

"I guess I'll just have to wait and see what happens."

"You might just surprise yourself.

"I hope it will be a good surprise. Until we talk again, then."

"Ciao for now, my friend..."

36. The Way of Passion

Sunday, September 17, 2017

"Good morning, Padre. Wrote a poem this morning called 'O, Oriana!' It's my distilled impressions of Oriana Fallaci's book *The Egoists*. I had to get those feelings out of my system, the wandering ego looking for its soul, always seeking to be more than it can ever be; that's the tragic feeling I got from reading about the egoists that Fallaci interviewed over the years and which she compiled into her book *The Egoists*. And I was left wondering, is it worth the bother?"

"If you're asking if life is worth the bother, ask yourself. Was it worth the bother?"

"Insomuch that I found my lost soul, yes; it was worth the bother, though I'd never repeat my life. Good God, what a journey!"

"Every life is a journey, and it will not end until one finds their lost soul. Yes, everyone is on a journey to their wholeness and completeness, and they will not stop until they arrive at their destination. This was the premise of your book The Pearl of Great Price. *You know the journey. You've lived it. Give the world a chance. It can be disappointing to see so much wasted time and energy, but life is, as you like to say, an individual journey; to which I will add, a journey to peace and understanding. And every soul will get there eventually. That's written in their spiritual DNA. So, what else is bothering you today?"*

"I started watching the TV series *Medici: Masters of Florence* yesterday evening and didn't go to bed until 1:30 because it brought back memories of my past lifetime in Italy when I was married to Penny whose heart I broke because of my love for my mistress; but I have to tell you, watching this series shortly after watching two seasons of *Outlander*, I feel like the karmic stupidity of man will never stop, and I say this because man is ruled by passion and not reason; that's the impression these two historical dramas have left me with."

"And you wouldn't be wrong in your impressions. Your past lifetime as a rich textile merchant was definitely a life of passion, for which you paid dearly in your current lifetime; but without passion, where would man be? Soul is born of passion, and soul-making is what man is born to do. We all come into life to grow in our own soul. This is what life is for. So, these historical dramas are good for the vicarious experience. They give the viewer an insight into the mystery of soul-making, despite how difficult some life experiences can be."

"The way of passion, then? That's how souls are made? The more passion we have for life, the more we grow spiritually? Is that the gist of it?"

"As simple as it sounds, yes. This is why people of passion can be so full of spirit. They generate the energy they need to become what they are meant to be, and it doesn't matter what kind of passion—good or bad, there's no morality to passion. It's the desire for more life, for more experience, for more self-identity. This is the natural way of life. That's what pulled you into the historical drama Outlander, *and that's what intrigues you about* The Medici. *You know them well, my friend; you were one of them. You belonged to the nobility of the rich, and you grew through your great passion for more life. You had to have what you desired, and you grew in your desires until you could take no more life. You died unresolved, but you died with the definite purpose that you were born for—to devour all the life you could before you died. That was your contract with life in that lifetime. And your contract in this lifetime was to find your lost soul. You found it, and here we are. That's why you changed the title of this book of dialogues from* Earth to Padre *to the new working title* Alone, But Never Alone. *Is that not so?"*

"Yes. I wanted to reflect the reality of my situation. I am very much alone, but I cannot ever get lonely again because I made the two into one and became my true self. I am what I am not and I am not what I am, I am both but neither; I am Soul. That's my reality. But God, do I feel out of context in life. I'm a stranger in a world of lost souls. But I don't like the sound of that. It sounds too much, if you know what I mean. But how can I explain it any simpler?"

"Do you have to? Just let it be. Live, love, and enjoy your life. You need not to do more."

"And write and write and write?"

A Sign of Things to Come

"Yes. Write to your heart's content."

"Penny just invited me out for breakfast. So, Padre; thank you for the chat. We're going out for breakfast, and then we have to get a new tank for our goldfish because his tank is leaking, and we have to pick up a new coffee pot because it's going on the blink. Our bread-maker died on me Friday too, and we're going to look for a new one today. Also, I have to pick up another gallon of paint to finish painting my writing room. Until we talk again, then."

"Have a lovely day, my friend..."

37. On the Discovery of a New Poet

Thursday, September 21, 2017

"Good morning, Padre. I want to share with you my discovery of a new poet, but before I do I have to ask you something. I want to know what's going on with my dreams. I woke up yesterday from some dreams that left me in a funny space, and I had to fight to concentrate my focus and get my life centered again. I managed to focus my energy enough through reading for an hour or so, and then I did some work on my writing room, getting the other two walls ready for painting; and this morning I woke up again from some dreams, and I feel I have to ask you: are my dreams affecting my consciousness? Affecting how I feel about myself? I dreamt of my family last night, one of those house dreams in which I am not welcomed like a son or sibling, which makes me feel apart from my family. Is this dream telling me something I need to know about myself? Or is it telling me something about my family?"

"Both. But before we begin, let me bid you good morning. You were right to glance at your book The Man of God Walks Alone, *because this book is one of your best. It speaks to your life like none of your other books, and this new book of dialogues is its sequel; so, let me answer your questions about your dreams. They are compensatory dreams to balance out your apprehensions about your life and your family. You miss your family connections on a deep level. Consciously, you are done with your family; but unconsciously you still miss your family. And when you dream of your family you wake up feeling at a loss. But it is not permanent. Family energy does one good, but you had to make a point with your family, and you made it. You had to teach your family the lesson of integrity. Your family is a proud, vain family; and it was up to you to break the cycle of vanity that your family is caught in. Now, what about this new poet?"*

Her name is Jane Hirshfield. Let me quote a poem that she inspired just to see if I got her correctly. I feel that she is walking in the shadow of Emily Dickinson, as close as she can come to solving the puzzle of the secret way, but not quite there yet. Here's my poem:

JANE, ZEN, AND POETRY

She almost has "it" but does not quite
know it, another experience, another
poem, another nanometer closer to "it."
Something she said gave her away:
"Most of the time I feel as if I am
in service of the poem," but not until
she sees that "it" is in equal service
of her will she have "it" and be
whole and complete.

"You caught the soul of her path, and you are correct to say that she's not quite there yet; but very, very close. Yes, she is an excellent poet with a deep insight into the secret way; but not until she sees that the secret way is life in all of its manifestations will she catch up to Emily Dickinson and walk alongside her. Read her poetry. It will help you with your own."

"Let's pursue this a moment. I've listened to Jane recite her poems and talk about her poetry and the art of writing poetry, and she's very insightful, much more insightful than other poets who talk about the mysterious nature of poetry, and I know that she sees the secret way of life; but still, she hasn't quite taken that last step that she needs to cross over into the realty of wholeness and completeness. Has this anything to do with her Zen Buddhist beliefs?"

"It does. She hasn't grasped the central point about the secret way, which is to individuate the consciousness of God. She will never grasp it as long as she clings to her Zen Buddhist beliefs. The self is individual and autonomous, and the secret way of life impels the self to wholeness and completeness. It is the purpose of life. This is a very difficult concept to grasp, and it stumbles every soul that seeks to solve the mystery of life. The self is the mystery, and until one sees that the self is the I of God in the process of realizing its divine nature will the mystery be solved. The I of God is the answer to all these nagging questions. But that's an individual journey, and every soul

must resolve this mystery in its own way. Some do so by becoming poets, others by becoming priests or doctors; whatever one does to solve this mystery, it has to be in service of life. The attitude of service to life is the answer to this mystery. Just as the secret way of life is in service of the individuation of the soul, so too must the individuating soul be in service of life. This is the mystery that faces the poet Jane Hirshfield. She's impaired by her own beliefs, as vast and expansive as they may be. She has to step out of the paradigm of Zen Buddhism to be set free.

"Let's talk about suffering. My understanding of suffering differs from the Buddhists. I do realize that suffering is born of our own ignorance, but I also see suffering as nature's way of resolving the longing in our soul for wholeness and completeness. This is at odds with most, if not all other teachings. I do not see suffering as the tragedy that others see it, and I cannot point my finger at God like most people do when they suffer, because I no longer see suffering as unfair and cruel. It may be cruel, but that's just the way life works. What do you have to say? After all, Padre; you suffered more than most any other person in the world with your stigmata; so, I know that you have an insight into suffering that is special. Which reminds me of what you said about suffering. If I'm not mistaken, you called suffering your glory, and you wished you could suffer more for your Lord Jesus. Am I correct in my memory?"

"You are. Yes, I did have a special insight into suffering; and it pleases me that you have caught the mystery of suffering. You expressed it differently, but essential you are correct to say that suffering is nature's way of resolving the longing in one's soul for wholeness and completeness. This is not what the Buddhists believe. They do not believe in the individual self, so how can they resolve the longing in their soul for wholeness and completeness? They have taken the way of non-being to the self, and that is a difficult path to take because it goes against the natural imperative of life to individuate the soul of man. This is the Buddhist dilemma, and the poet Jane Hirshfield's dilemma. Her poetry is deep, but it doesn't resolve the longing in one's soul; it merely resolves the quandaries of life. To get to the deep mystery of the self, the paradox of the being and non-being of life has to be resolved. You did, that's why you see

104

life differently. This is why it is vital for you to write and write and write."

"Now, the big issue: my energy, my consciousness, my feelings. I want to know what is going on. Am I on another down cycle?"

"You are. You have been going down for a while now, but that's just the way life works. Your down cycle is almost over and you will be on an up cycle within a few days. Once you start on your up cycle you will see life differently. Don't' fret, my friend; just do what you are doing, and try to focus your energies on doing. DOING is your ticket home."

"I like that. Well, I hope to do some painting today. I want to finish my writing room so I can get it in order. This will please Penny. I want to make it as clutter free as possible so she can vacuum the room when she vacuums the house. Before, I had it all cluttered with boxes in front of my book shelves, and papers here and there, all collecting dust. It wasn't chi-flowing, if you know what I mean. So, I'm doing some *feng shui* on my writing room."

"And you will see the difference. You also have to clean out the closet and organize it for you papers and manuscripts. That will go a long way in your feng shui-ing."

"I miss my water-drinking discipline. I have to get it back. Five to six glasses a day, and I would like to do my stationary bike for fifteen minutes a day. I need a boost, Padre."

"Start today. I will be there for you."

"Thank you. Until we talk again…"

38. On the Philosophy of No-self

Friday, September 22, 2017

"Good morning, Padre. We picked up our car BEWEL from the body shop yesterday and we're glad to have it back. It's been quite a little ordeal, the accident and all the inconvenience; but that's life, isn't it? I hope we can have some normalcy now. I finished painting my writing room yesterday, and today I'm going to put my books back in the book cases. It'll be nice to be clutter-free. Now I can be proud of my writing room. I think I did a little *feng shui-ing* in the room and the Chi should flow more freely. What do you think?"

"A clutter-free writing room is very important. Yes, feng shui-ing your room will do your writing a lot of good. It will also be clutter free now. If only you could see how clutter free your writing will be from here on in. I promise that your life is on a different turn."

"A good one, I hope."

"Of course. I wouldn't promise you any other turn."

"I'm warming up to work on my new spiritual musing, 'Sharon's Comeuppance.' I started it yesterday and worked on it throughout the day as I painted my room. I hope to have it done within a few days. I want to post it next Saturday. I don't quite know where it's going, but I enjoyed the part I wrote so far. It brings together the two forces of life—the disruptive force and the harmonizing force. Sharon is Murphy's nasty sister and symbolizes the disruptive force of life, and synchronicity symbolizes the harmonizing force. I hope I can work out the logic of these two forces."

"You will. Just go with your muse. It will guide you."

"Do we invite Sharon's disruptive forces into our life?"

"The short answer is yes. You must remember that life is made up of the enantiodromiac pull of these two forces. They are in constant play. This is how soul grows and individuates."

"Should I pursue this issue of the no-self? I feel I have a big musing coming on."

A Sign of Things to Come

"It is necessary, and you will write your spiritual musing on the no-self. You have a unique perspective on the self, and you must get this across."

"Here's a question: to what purpose, this philosophy of no-self?"

"To what purpose anything? Life is its own purpose, to individuate the I of God. And how it does this is life's logic. The question central to the philosophy of no-self is this: why am I not what I am? Until one can answer that question one will never break free of the hold the philosophy of no-self has upon them."

"I can only speak for myself. It's taken me a long time to answer that question, and I did to my satisfaction. I think I understand now why you encouraged me to always go back to my own beliefs, because in my beliefs I am most confident; and my beliefs of the individuation process as I experienced it gives me the confidence to write a spiritual musing on the philosophy of no-self, which I believe hampers soul's journey of self-discovery; so I think I will write a spiritual musing on the subject. I may write a poem first, though."

"By all means, write a poem and a spiritual musing on the subject of no-self. It will do your readers a lot of good. Write it with your own personal beliefs underlying the theme. This will give your poem and musing the credibility the reader needs to see the whole picture."

"How did the philosophy of no-self originate?"

"It was born of the shadow, the non-being aspect of soul's consciousness. Once the I of God got trapped in the non-being consciousness of the soul, it created a whole philosophy to justify itself. Such is how the shadow thinks. It needs to be, even if it is a no-self. That's the irony of this philosophy. It isn't a self, but it wants to be a self, and being a no-self is the closest it can get; and so, the game goes on with few people ever seeing through the irony."

"It seems that a lot of nice people get trapped by this philosophy. I'm thinking of the new poet that I just discovered. Jane Hirshfield. She's a very nice lady, but her Zen philosophy has got her bound to this philosophy of no-self, and that's inhibiting her individuation; isn't it?"

"Yes, very much. She suffers in her philosophy; but that's the path she was called to, and she lives it with authenticity. That's what

Orest Stocco

makes it tragic. Just as you lived that new age spiritual teaching for over thirty years. You lived it with authenticity, and it did serve you well; but you had to break away once it had served its purpose. She too must break away one day. Perhaps her poetry will help her, but that's her choice."

"Okay, Padre; I should get on with my writing. I want to read some musings to see which one I'm going to post on my blog tomorrow, and maybe I'll work on my new musing. Thank you for chatting this morning. Until we talk again, my friend."

"Ciao for now..."

39. She Wants More Padre

Monday, September 25, 2017

"Good morning, Padre. I meant to chat with you yesterday but never got around to it. I wanted to tell you that Sharon finished reading my novel *Healing with Padre Pio*, and her comment about the book was, 'I want more.' She wants a sequel, Padre; but I don't think I will be working on that this year. I was hoping to, but life got in the way. Will we ever write a sequel to this novel? I would love to, because there's a lot I want to discuss with you."

"We will, and there will be a lot to discuss. The journey from your book Healing with Padre Pio *to its sequel has been very fulfilling for you, given the number of books that you have written since, and what we will be discussing will take you into deeper truths, the truths you have been intimating with your musings. I look forward to working with you and your medium again."*

"I have a big thought in the back of my mind, a thought that is gestating into an idea for a spiritual musing, a thought that wants to give expression to what feels like the natural path of life which can simply be called 'the gnostic way.' I don't have the creative energy for that musing right now, and I know it would take my best creative energies to work it out, but what is this big thought all about anyway?"

"It's about the way. You will be rendering all spiritual paths to the personal way, which your muse has called 'the gnostic way.' This will put a lot of readers at ease about spiritual paths, and I look forward to reading it."

"Yesterday after I picked up my *Sunday Star* at Jug City in Waverley I looked in my car to see if I had a copy of my book *Why Bother? The Riddle of the Good Samaritan* to bring to Sharon because she had asked me on Saturday what book of mine she should read next, and I did have one copy; so, I drove to her place and gave her the book. I was nudged to bring her that book."

"That's the logical order for her. After reading Healing with Padre Pio, *she needs to know what she can do to answer the question why bother?"*

"Which brings me to professor Harold Bloom's book *Till I End My Song, A Gathering of Last Poems* which I was looking at on Amazon this morning. I read his introduction and was brought to dry tears by his concluding paragraph; I say dry tears, because I cannot shed wet tears for Harold Bloom anymore. I did when I heard one of his interviews. His bittersweet despair made me cry. So, I'd like to quote the concluding paragraph of his introduction to what he considers to be last poems:

"No one not far from eight relishes the forms and accents of farewell. Yet, for the secular, who rejects illusion, where else is consolation to be found? In the view of its gatherer, this volume does not propose any exaltation of the spirit, but I am a critic and teacher, not a poet. Intimations of immortality collide with resigned skepticisms throughout this book. Confronting illness, pain, and dying, we learn quickly that eloquence is not enough. Neither are even the most authentic poems of consolation. Still, the beauty and wisdom of these poems reverberate in the coming silence."

"He wrote this in June, 2010. He's still alive, but I doubt that he has broken through the thick wall of his secular illusion—if I may be so humorous. There's a sadness to his perspective on life that really does make me cry inside. I honestly feel sorry for the man. I love his passion for life, but his nihilism, as breathtaking as it may be, saddens me."

"He is a good and wise man and he will find his way out of his own darkness eventually, but that's his personal journey. You understand him better than most people, and you captured the soul of the man in several of your poems, but there's nothing you can do about him. Let go and let God; that's the only solution to another soul's journey."

"Sorry, Padre; I have to run. We may pick this up another time."

"Okay, my friend. Until we talk again…"

40. Alone, but Never Lonely

Saturday, September 30, 2017

"Good morning, Padre. Last night Penny and I watched a movie on Netflix called *Our Souls at Night*, starring Robert Redford and Jane Fonda, and it's about a widow who asks a widower neighbor if he would like to sleep with her because she gets very lonely at night. He accepts her offer; and, of course, the story lets us in on their personal history, and eventually they do become intimate. I mention this movie because I want to talk to you about loneliness, something that I no longer experience. Are you up to a little chat on loneliness this morning?"

"You couldn't have chosen a more relevant topic to talk about, because loneliness is man's private heartache. No one can escape it. I know you have transcended this basic human emotion because you brought your two selves into one and no longer long to be whole and complete, but you are the exception. Loneliness is both man's curse and blessing. It is man's blessing, because loneliness compels man to seek wholeness and completeness, which is temporarily satisfied in the company of others as Robert and Jane do in the movie by sleeping together; and it is man's curse because loneliness can drive one to despair, the most depressing emotion. Now, perhaps we should talk about solutions to loneliness. That's what I spent most of my time on when I heard confessions, bestowing upon my penitents the gift of purpose. What are your thoughts, if I may ask to engage the spirit of this morning's talk?"

"My thoughts? I agree, one must have a purpose to live for; otherwise one gets sucked into the wasteland of emptiness, that vast terrain of meaninglessness that colors everything absurd. But can't that lead to a false perspective on life, as it did with Sartre and Camus and every other existentialist who could not resolve the meaning and purpose of man's existence? They tried to posit meaning and purpose to life by the engagement of free will, but ultimately it did not resolve the issue of man's purpose for being; it only forestalled it."

"Exactly. Man is free to choose his life, but does the life he chooses resolve the issue of his destined purpose? That's the question they could never answer, because they never penetrated the secret of man's destined purpose. How could they when they negated God, and by consequence the divine sparks of God, which every soul is? This is a subject that we should pursue, because man needs to hear the call to his destined purpose."

"I'd really like to oblige, Padre; but, in all honesty, I'm a little tired. Nay, I'm sick and tired of trying to get the point across that we are here for the purpose of realizing our true self, because no one wants to hear this stuff. The world is too caught up in itself. Man doesn't want to hear what I have to say, so why bother? Who am I, anyway? Just a voice in the wilderness of Tiny Township, Georgian Bay, Ontario; a voice crying in the dark. But no one's listening, no one cares; so why bother with these talks, with my writing? You know what I'm getting at, don't you? For example, I just posted a new spiritual musing on my blog this morning. It's called 'The Bread Maker Coincidence and Sharon's Comeuppance,' and perhaps thirty, maybe forty people will view this musing, and then it will disappear into the oblivion of the ethers; so, I ask again, why bother trying to wake people up to their destined purpose?"

"Do you remember the story of the starfish? Remember the moral of the story, 'It matters to this starfish'? That's why you should bother, because there may be one person who reads your blog and takes it to heart. As I've told you time and again, you do not choose your readers; they choose you, and it's up to you to be there for them to choose. Capisce?"

"*Capisce?* You dare to ask me if I understand? Of course, I understand; but why should I care? What difference does it make if I affect one reader with my writing when they will get there eventually, because that's just the way life works. If not me, someone else; and I'm tired of the efforts that I put into my writing—sorry, Padre; that's my purpose. That's what gives my life meaning through the wasteland of life's absurdity. I didn't mean this self-pity. I must consolidate my energies and focus on my intention, which is how I transcended my loneliness in the first place; so, perhaps we should talk about INTENTION?"

A Sign of Things to Come

"It took you a while, but you got there. Yes, intention is what we should focus on, because without intention one has no purpose, and without purpose one gets bored and listless, which breeds loneliness and despair. So, what do you have to say about intention?"

"Intention is purpose-driven. Intention is goal-oriented. Intention gives one the will to do, and doing is what you are driving at, isn't it? Because for you DOING is the answer to most of life's problems. The more one *does,* the more one will *be*; and the more one *is,* the less lonely they will be, because loneliness is directly proportional to one's non-being. Meaning, the more one is centered in their non-being, the lonelier they will be because they will be caught in the consciousness of what they are not, which is the central mystery of loneliness. How's that for a metaphysical explanation for this dreaded topic of loneliness? But who cares? Who will understand that we are both what we are and what we are not, and to overcome our loneliness we have to become more of what we are and less of what we are not? That's how I overcame my loneliness—and believe me, I was lonely! I was the loneliest man in the world when I went on my quest for my true self. How else could I have come up with the saying, 'The shortest way to God is through hell," and by hell I meant the wasteland of my own shadow. So, Padre; what do you have to say about that? Loneliness is man's hell, because man is what he is not; and not until he reconciles his non-being with his being will he cease to be lonely. End of story."

"I guess that puts me in my place."

"Alright, don't be funny. You know I had to get that off my chest. That's what bothers me about my writing: it's too much for my readers. That's my curse—"

"And blessing. Your capacity for expressing the paradoxical nature of man's becoming is a marvel you should and will one day be acknowledged for, so don't give up on yourself. Just keep writing your spiritual musings, your poetry, and stories; they will find their place. Trust me, my friend; I see the big picture from here."

"And? Can you share the big picture with me?"

"Not yet, but one day I will. Anything else you would like to say about loneliness?"

"I'll give the last word to you, if you don't mind."

"No, I don't mind. My last word on loneliness for today would be this: to break the hold that loneliness has upon you, find something to do and lose yourself in the doing. The doing will generate the energy of purpose, and the more purpose-energy one has the less lonely they will be. That's the secret to overcoming loneliness. Do, do, and do some more. Always find something to do to keep your mind busy from thinking about yourself. Lose yourself in the doing. That's the quick fix solution. The long fix solution will come to you eventually, because as I said the energy of doing is purpose-energy, and all purpose-energy nourishes the self; and you know that the more self one has, the less empty one will be. That's my last word for today."

"What did you think of today's spiritual musing?"

"Beautiful. It was simple and profound. You gave the reader much to think about."

"Thanks, Padre. I can always count on you. Until we talk again."

"Have a wonderful day, my friend..."

41. Like a Fly Flitting on Water

Wednesday, October 4, 2017

"Good morning, Padre. I feel like a fly flitting upon the surface of water, one moment here another moment there, never stopping long enough to savor the moment, and I feel a disconnect with my source of inspiration, and I wonder what I can do about it."

"You have been flitting lately, but that is not a bad thing. You have worked yourself thin in your writing and painting and need time to replenish your energies. Don't fret, my friend; your creative well is filling as we speak"

"I have to tell you something. Yesterday Sharon came over for a visit and we talked about my last spiritual musing ('A Very Big Thought'), which I printed up and read to her, and then about my novel *Healing with Padre Pio,* which she could not get enough of; that's why the book left her feeling like she wanted more. That's what she said, and I regret not getting in touch with the psychic who channeled you for my novel so we could work on a sequel. What happened, Padre? Did life get in the way again? That's why I didn't initiate the project, isn't it?"

"You had too much on your plate. At least, Penny did. No, you weren't ready yet to get involved in writing a sequel, which would have taken you deep into the mysteries; but you will get it started when the time is ready, which will be sooner than you think. I will be here, waiting to work with you, and we will give your friend all she needs to satisfy her longing for more. But in the meantime, continue with your writing. You will come upon some literature very soon that will absorb you and keep you involved. It's just around the corner."

"Okay, let's talk about my dismay with my writing and books in general. I don't seem to get what I used to get from the books I'm reading, nor from my own writing even, and this is beginning to disconcert me. What's going on?"

"You're in transition from one state of consciousness to another. It's only natural for you, given that you have initiated your own process of individuation."

"Which brings me to the question of authenticity. I'm beginning to see just how meshed the shadow is with the ego personality, and I'm getting a whole new perspective on the enantiodromiac process of man's becoming, and it's giving me a greater insight as to why man cannot see his own falseness; it's much too much a part of his personality to see it."

"Exactly true. This was my realization in my lifetime as the Holy Confessor. I began to see just how difficult it was for my penitents to see their own sinful self because it was so much a part of who they were, and it took a lot of prayers for me to break the hold that my own mind had upon me, because I had to see my own falseness first, just as you have done and continue to do; and I don't mind telling you how proud I am of your journey to peace and understanding."

"What about all the little troubles we had in our life this past few months? What was that all about, anyway?"

"Just making room for more growth and understanding."

"Will Penny and I ever have the peace and quiet and anxiety-free time to enjoy the rest of our life together?"

"Very much so. It's just around the corner."

"That's one hell of a big corner, don't you think?"

"It's shorter than you think, my friend."

"I hope so, because I'd love nothing more than for us enjoy the rest of our life together with peace of mind. That's my wish."

"Granted."

"Is there anything else you wish to say to me this morning?"

"Don't look for your inspiration. It's there waiting for you. Just go about your day, flitting from one place to another until you land where you are meant to land. Then you can savor the moment and enjoy your next project. Have a nice day, my friend."

"Thank you, Padre…"

42. A Thanksgiving Story

Monday, October 9, 2017

"Good morning, Padre. It's been quite a Thanksgiving weekend, and it's not over yet. It won't be over until Penny gets home. She's in Ottawa where she went for her niece's wedding and should be at the airport now with her two sisters waiting for a flight to Toronto, and then Penny will take the Go Transit and I will pick her up at the station in Barrie. She's going to phone and give me the details so I'll know what time to pick her up; but it's been quite a weekend, because it was fraught with curious interruptions. First, the Go Train from Barrie to Toronto was cancelled when I brought her Friday morning because of an incident on or at the Go Train (someone committed suicide), and she had to take a bus to Toronto, which barely got her there on time to catch her flight to Ottawa, but she did make it. However, her luggage did not arrive, and her new dress for the wedding was in her luggage. The wedding was the next day, so she was going to have to go shopping for a new dress and shoes and whatever else she needed; but her sister-in-law and mother of the bride, with whom she had a falling out ever since Penny and I got together offered Penny one of her dresses because they were the same size, and her sister-in-law apologized to her for treating her the way she did all those years; but her luggage came in Saturday morning in time for the wedding at four o'clock so she had her own new dress to wear, which brought the incident to a happy resolution. Which led me to wonder if that whole thing wasn't choreographed so Penny and her sister-in-law could make up their differences. What do you say about that, Padre; was it choreographed?"

"It certainly had the hand of God in it, of that I am certain. Yes, it was choreographed as you say, but there were other factors involved. The experience was for everyone, and it precipitated her ex-husband's heart attack, which added to the drama. And as to her Master Card getting compromised later in the day, that was also choreographed by the invisible Hand of God for reasons which were

a healing benefit for everyone in Penny's family. It was indeed a thanksgiving weekend for everyone, but especially for Penny."

"I would really like to write a short story on this weekend. I would even like to call it 'A Thanksgiving Story.' Will I ever get to write it, because I'm feeling spiritless now; and by that, I mean that I seem to have flame of my creative fire."

"Your flame is burning low, but it will burn high and hot and with much more creative intensity than before once you re-connect with your creative self. You have taken a break and will do so for another few weeks, and then you will reconnect and start fresh. Yes, you will write a story on this weekend's drama, and it will be one of your best stories. Trust me."

"I hope so, because this has all the elements of a wonderful story which I hope to write in a different style. I hope so, anyway."

"You will. It will be a combination of Hemingway and Munro, two of your favorite writers, with a little John Updike thrown in; but it will be your own voice, your own style. It will be one of your breakthrough stories."

"I visited Sharon the other day, the lady who has taken to my books and moved by them and who follows my musings on my blog, and she called me yesterday to tell me that she read my last spiritual musing 'The Essence of Cool' and didn't quite get it, so she wanted me to explain it to her, or give her an instance of what it meant to be cool. I did, pointing out that the cool person (like Paul Newman in the movie *Cool Hand Luke*) is someone who doesn't follow the crowd and does his/her own thing, someone who marches to the beat of his own drum, and then she got it and thanked me for explaining; but my question is, are my musings becoming too abstruse?"

"On the contrary, your spiritual musings are taking on a special kind of clarity that speaks to the new way of thinking that you are introducing to the world through your writing. Your spiritual musings must be read two or three times to get the point you make, because your point is so well reasoned and the reader has to re-think how they perceive life. That's the effect your musings have on your reader. Keep writing your spiritual musings. They are good for you and your readers. They speak in the language of your understanding of the way, which is so penetrating that it gets to the very core of

man's being. Your musings speak to the meaning and purpose of life, which make them very powerful reading."

"I've felt the change in how my spiritual musings are written now, a gradual change into a new kind of clarity that speaks to the individual in a new way. I can't explain it just yet, but it seems to me that I am speaking to my reader from the essence of my own life experience, which says that I have found my own writer's voice, which is quite different from any writer that I have ever read. Am I correct in this perception?"

"Indeed, you are. Your voice is coming to the fore, and it will only get stronger as you write. This is why you must write your stories."

"Padre, I'd love to have a creatively productive winter, free of anxieties. Can you help me make that happen? I want to get some of my work completed and new work started. I need to bring my life's work to resolution."

"And it shall be. Keep up your end of the work and I'll take care of the anxiety part of your life. Work, write and write and write; that's all I ask of you."

"Then I'd better start fanning the flame of my creative fire!"

"Yes, my friend; fan the flame and let the fire burn and burn and burn and you will bring resolution to your life's work. I promise."

"Thank you, Padre."

"You're welcome…"

43. Oh No, a Directive from My Muse!

Sunday, October 15, 2017

"Good morning, Padre. Let me get right to it. I need your advice. I just got a directive from my muse while sipping herbal tea with Penny on our front deck this morning, and as I read my *Sunday Star* I told Penny that I had just finished reading the most comprehensive biography on Gurdjieff called *The Harmonious Circle, The Lives and Works of G. I. Gurdjieff, P. D. Ouspensky and Their Followers,* by James Webb, and an idea was forming in my mind for a spiritual musing; and then, out of the blue I got an inner directive to write a short book instead called *The Gnostic Way of Life*, and I have to ask your advice on this because I hate it when I'm called away from other writing projects that I have planned and ready to go. So, Padre; what do you say?"

"I say that you should listen to your muse. Your muse did not give you a directive to write this book to pull you away from your other projects, because your muse did not know that this new project was in the offing; you brought it about by the last spiritual musing that you were called to write—"

"You mean my spiritual musing 'The Stick with Two Ends, Shania Twain and P. D. Ouspensky,' which came to me out of the blue also?"

*"Yes. Because of what your spiritual musing brought forth, the idea for a literary essay on the gnostic way of life arose; that's why your muse gave you a strong directive to write a narrative essay on the gnostic way of life and why you reacted so strongly at the thought because you hate being pulled away from other projects. My advice is to listen to your muse, because **your creative unconscious is your gnostic way. It is your path, your secret way of life.**"*

"Wow! So, there it is then?"

"Yes."

"And of course, my theme would be the natural process of individuation to wholeness and completeness through life experience, which would be the gnostic way of life?"

"Yes. Your connection with the creative principle would be your point of entry. Where it takes you, only your muse can say."

"And you think I should go ahead with it?"

"The sooner the better."

"Alright, I'm going to open a new file as soon as we finish chatting. I want to ask you something else. This past few weeks have been rather trying, Penny's trip to Ottawa for her niece's wedding and all the surprising circumstances that ensued; there's more to this story than I can see, and I've seen behind the scenes because Penny's whole experience spoke to the redemptive principle of life, the power of a higher frequency energy affecting everyone at the wedding ceremony. Am I correct in this perception?"

"Yes, and you should write a story on this whole episode. You must take your notes on the experience before it fades into the back of your mind."

"Before or after I start my narrative essay on the gnostic way of life?"

"After. You are engaged with the idea now, so take advantage of it. Your reading of James Webb's biography is fresh on your mind, and that's what inspired your essay on the gnostic way of life; so, get your new book started. Once started, you will be on your way."

"Okay, but I'm holding you responsible for this new book."

"I will gladly shoulder the responsibility. Get started then, with my blessing."

"Okay. Thank you, Padre."

"You're welcome…"

44. Don't Know What to Say

"Well, Padre; I don't know what to say. Here we go again, the tenants of the top unit of our triplex have given notice and will be out by the end of November; they are moving to Thunder Bay. They are a young couple, but he was laid off from his job and they're moving to the city because the job prospects are better there. Now Penny and I have the worry of finding tenants. We've been here before, and it's not a nice place to be. It may not seem like a big deal, but it is in a lot of little ways; and as you know, little worries become big anxieties. Can you console me?"

"Yes, little worries can become big anxieties; but you have no need to worry. This is all part of the bigger picture. Give it a few days to settle down and let the energies find their level, and then things will look a lot better. I'm taking the matter into hand."

"I'm anxious enough to precipitate a heart attack, you know that?"

"It's not your time yet. Sit back, read, and relax."

"I wish I could let go and let God; but I can't let go. It's gotten hold of me, like a pesky little demon. But for some reason, I've been expecting this."

"It was in the offing. The young couple have their destined purpose also. Just let go and I'll take care of it for you. Don't worry. Things will turn out better than before."

"We should have lowered the price of the triplex in the spring. It might have sold."

"Yes, it might have. You can try lowering it now, offering the top unit to entice a buyer because they will have a place to stay. Run it by your realtor."

"I'm not feeling so good. I think I'm going to have a panic attack thinking about our triplex, the work that needs to be done on it, the coming winter, the worry. Get us a buyer, please. I'm so sorry for beseeching you this way, but where else can I turn?"

A Sign of Things to Come

"Please sit down in your chair and close your eyes."
"I'm going to do that."
"Good. Leave the rest to me."
"Thank you, Padre…"

"It's 3 A. M. and I can't sleep. I took a sleeping pill around 7:30 and I'm up now. I can't get the worry out of my head. I made a big mistake with our triplex. I should have insisted on a lower price for the sale, but I had to please Penny; now I don't think we can sell it. I'm going to reduce the sale by twenty thousand and see what happens. Any advice?"

"Don't panic. Yes, reduce the price; but don't panic. It will find a sale."

"We need a tenant for the winter."

"Yes. That will happen."

"I'm sorry. I've never felt like this before, or have I?"

"Many times. But being older, you feel it more acutely now."

"I'm scared, Padre. I've never admitted this before. I'm scared for Penny. I could have done so much better for her. I failed to do her the right she deserved, and now I question my whole writing life. Would my life have been better had I not written those two novels that severed us from our community?"

"It would have been better financially, perhaps; but it certainly would not have allowed you to achieve what you came into this world to achieve. You could not have done that in your hometown. That was why you had to be severed from there. Your life is the life that you had to live to achieve the outcome that you did."

"Tell me, what outcome was that?"

"You broke the cycle of your karmic life and realized your spiritual self. You came back to live your life over again to give birth to your spiritual self. You have achieved that. Now you are writing about your experience. This is your destined purpose."

"And all this damn worry?"

"It was necessary. Now it is becoming a burden and it will be taken care of."

"How? When? I'm tired, Padre; really tired. I could die of a heart attack any day now."

"It's not your time. You have many books to write yet."

"I'm tired of being under the gun. Please put my mind at ease."

"Sit back, read, relax, and drift off to sleep..."

45. My Demon Fears

Friday, November 3, 2017

"Good morning, Padre. Am I going to have a heart attack? I feel like I'm going to. I need your immediate attention. Have I got it, or am I slipping into some fantasy world out of desperation? What's going on? Please tell me."

"You are in a state of anxiety brought on by your own demon fears. You have to stop worrying about something that will never happen. You have let yourself slip into a worry that isn't necessary, because your circumstances don't warrant this kind of worry. You are so much better off than you think that you fear slipping into a state that you cannot repair, but this state is so far away from your circumstances that it is not possible to fall so far. Your worries are a dread because you cannot get them out of your own head. How many times I had to comfort my penitents about their worries. And they did have worries. But always I prayed and asked them to pray. This was my constant refrain. Pray, hope, and don't worry my friend. God is with you."

"I've come too far to lose it now, Padre. I have to see this through. How?"

"Lose yourself in your writing. Write and write and write and plan more writing. Do what you have to do for your winter duties. Clean your yard of leaves and cut down some trees. You will have enough firewood for what you need. Write. That's your cure."

"And what about our triplex?"

"Let it go for the new price. It's set in motion now. Don't worry. It's going to happen."

"I do want to write. I do want to get this new book finished. I'm not half way there yet, but I know it's on its way. I just wrote another chapter yesterday and I think it's good. It's called 'The Way Is an Open Secret.' I didn't expect it to come out the way it did. And I started a new chapter called 'Acquiring a Center of Gravity.' I don't know how it's going to go, but I want to work on it today. I do feel better when I am writing because I am focussed. But I have let my life get out of hand by not making decisions to take better care of Penny. I feel bad, Padre. I really do."

"You had too much on your plate and you did the best you could. You were born to find your lost soul, and you found it. That was your purpose in this life. Your life with Penny is going very well, and you are going into your senior years with grace. I promise you."

"I don't want to feel as desperate as I feel. It's hard on my heart."

"Lose yourself in your writing today. Just write and rest today. That's all you need to do to get yourself into a better frame of mind. Now let it go."

"I'm going to work on my writing now."

"Good. We can talk again later…

46. Cards on the Table

Tuesday, December 5, 2017

"Good morning, Padre. It's been a while since our last talk. I've been meaning to open up a dialogue, but for some reason kept putting it off. Now I have something to ask you: will Penny and I ever have some period of anxiety-free time so we can have some measure of happiness? I know that life is about change, but good God do we have to keep getting these little surprises that send us into depression? What's going on, Padre? Can we put our cards on the table?"

"There is a time for all seasons, and now you are going through a time of minor change; there is nothing to worry about. All is taken care of as we speak. Problems always look like mountains at first, but later they become molehills. Your problem is a molehill which will be resolved by the end of the week. Do not worry your head off."

"This did not have to occur. Why did it?"

"It's the blending of energies. Once they blend, they create a new frequency. It's all in the blending. It will be sorted out and all will be back to normal."

"What about our mental and emotional health? It's taking its toll on us."

"Your health is better than you think. You will survive this and be healthier for it."

"Can you give us a helping hand?"

"Certainly. I've already begun."

"Quiet, quiet, and more quiet time; that's all Penny and I want. A graceful retirement. We'd like to live our life enjoying our accomplishments, but anxiety keeps getting in the way. Why cannot we ever seem to get there, Padre? What's the hinderance?"

"You were born to achieve a different outcome, and you have achieved it; and now you are writing your story. That is your duty to yourself. And Penny chose to assist you in your life. You have accomplished much more than you both expected, and there is more

to come. I assure you, my friend, the heavens are conspiring to see your mission completed."

"Would you please calm our tenant down. She's afraid and upset. She needs your healing energy, Padre. Would you please embrace her and calm her anxiety?"

"I have done so. She will be fine, I promise."

"Penny got *My Writing Life* published on Lulu. We're expecting the proof copies to arrive in a week. I don't know about this book now. I feel a little odd."

"You feel that way after every book you write. My Writing Life *is an extraordinary book. It reveals more gnostic wisdom than many of your other books. Be proud of it."*

"And now I'm coming to the final chapters of *The Gnostic Way of Life.* I was going great guns until we got a call from our tenant about the water leak. Now we have to deal with that."

"Be of good cheer. It is in God's hands. I promise happy resolution."

"I read a couple of books about Jesus and the Essenes. I think they got it right, Jesus was an initiate of the Essenes, and I think his teaching has been watered down; that's what I'm trying to show with my writing. Padre, it's getting to the point where I don't want to go silent, but I can't, can I" I have to keep writing, don't I?"

"Yes. It is your duty to get it out. You have tapped into the Source. You are a knower. You have to write to let the world know the way as you have experienced it."

"Can you please, please, please find us a buyer for our triplex?"

"It's in God's hands, my friend. I promise a happy resolution."

"Will Penny and I be around to see it?"

"Certainly. You will have your graceful retirement. Once again, this is a promise that I will not break. It is my mission to see you through to the end of this life. We are together in this, my friend. We have much work to do yet."

"Which book after *The Gnostic Way of Life*? Get *The Armchair Guru* out?"

"Yes. Then Sparkles in the Mist. *And then a novel."*

"I'm think maybe *The Waking Dream* novel?"

"You certainly are ready to rework it."

"Can you see it from where you are?"

"Yes."

"Reworked?"

"Yes."

"And?"

"You did it justice, and it will be a wonderful read. Trust the process."

"Will I do my fictional Carl Jung justice?"

"Yes. He will guide you in the writing."

"Time's winged chariot is drawing near. Will I have time?"

"More than you need."

"What else is there to say?"

"Trust God, trust yourself, trust your readers. All is in good hands."

"Thank you…"

47. There's No End to Anxiety

Saturday, December 9, 2017

"Asking for one week without anxiety would be too much, but I'm thankful for what you said in our last talk; we got the toilet replaced in the top unit of our apartment complex and solved the leak problem, but now we have to deal with the stained ceiling tiles in the middle apartment, and the patio door issue. There's no end to our anxiety, Padre."

"Change is a way of life. This is not a disaster. It is the consequence of one action, and by the end of the week you will feel much better."

"Well we do feel a lot better this week than last week, but still Penny and I are getting worn down, to the point where Penny said she just doesn't care anymore. What am I to do?"

"Be patient. Like you said, you are being fine-tuned."

"Is there any truth to this? I was just being creative to appease her."

"You were right on the mark. Spiritual fine-tuning is what life is all about."

"Does it have to involve all of these anxieties?"

"On the whole, yes. Through solving life's problems, one tunes one's spirit."

"I posted a spiritual musing this morning. It's called "The Puzzled Father." I posted it as a Christmas parable. I wonder how it will go over."

"It's a beautiful story. Many will wonder about you now."

"In what way?"

"They will see that there is much more to you than they realize."

"But will they follow up on their curiosity?"

"Some will. Most will be afraid to."

"I've been watching YouTube interviews with the literary critic James Wood and listening to radio podcasts of Bookworm with

A Sign of Things to Come

Michael Silverblatt and I am amazed at their literary insights and knowledge, but ultimately they merely convince me that where I am they are trying to get to, and I wonder: am I wasting my time with these passionate lovers of literature?"

"No. You are learning of the limitations of literature and how they need to know more which they don't know how to seek. Keep learning from their ignorance. It confirms what you have found and gives you more confidence in your own writing."

"Will our new apartment issue be resolved soon?"

"Yes. Sooner than you think. Trust God, my friend. You are in God's hands, and all will unfold according to the Divine Plan of God. Nothing will ensue that will bother you. I promise."

I can count on you, Padre?"

"Always, my friend."

"Back to the literary critics and Bookworm host Michael Silverblatt; they are very erudite on literature, but they cannot break out of the paradigm. How do I respond to this?"

"Work it out in a spiritual musing."

"I've got one started. Is that the one to work it out in?"

"Yes. Work on it and see what happens."

"I will…"

48. Can't I Go One Week Without Anxiety?

Thursday, December 21, 2017

"Padre, can't I go one week without anxiety? Yesterday I was eating some Italian "honey balls" that Penny made for Christmas and one of my fillings fell out. They were hard and I had to chew and the pressure on my teeth must have forced the filling in one of my front teeth to loosen and fall out, and now I have to go to the dentist which I have been avoiding because a month or so ago another filling fell out, and I just hate going to the dentist; but I have no choice now, do I? I have to go to get my teeth fixed, and I'm not proud of that. I've been so damn neglectful that I felt like shit. I do, Padre. And this morning I discovered that we had a leak in the hot water line under our kitchen sink and I had to soak up the water in the cabinet under the sink and then I had to tighten the nut on the connecting line up to the faucet, and I hope that it will hold; but can't I have one week without anxiety? What the hell is going on, Padre?"

"It's your new frequency. Your life has been shaken up. This is how you expand your paradigm and grow in your wholeness."

"Wonderful. But good God, what a bloody nuisance. I need rest, Padre. I need some peace and quiet, some anxiety free time. If it's not our triplex, it's something else; never an end to all these little annoyances. Please, when can I get some anxiety-free time?"

"You shall have it very soon. I promise. Starting today."

"I'd like to believe you, I really would; but, how can I?"

"Place your trust in God. God will see to it that you have all the anxiety-free time to do your writing. Just do what you have to do and let go and let God."

"I wrote a poem yesterday, which today I have called 'The Way of Literature' (it was titled 'D.F.W. before I changed it this morning), inspired by the writer David Foster Wallace who took his own life in 2008 at the age of 45), and I wasn't very kind to him; but I wanted to show that his life was his path, and his path led him to suicide. Could he not have broken from his path and saved himself? Or was he pre-destined to kill himself?"

A Sign of Things to Come

"He was free to choose another path, but his mind was much too fast and busy for him to process all the information that he took in; that's why he killed himself. He wanted to stop sinking into depression which finally swallowed him. It was a spiritual choice, but existentially he was free to change the course of his life. He was too shadow-afflicted to do so. That's what lies at the heart of your poem. You captured his dilemma, though few people will see it."

"That poem shows my annoyance with life. Life can suck up the best of us and we can't seem to do anything about it, like D.F.W. That's why I wrote my poem."

"Life could have very easily sucked you up, but you broke the pattern that would have destroyed you. You did it, why not others? It's always a personal choice. That's what I kept telling the people who came to my confessional. Trust God, but make the effort. That's the answer. Write your books and let God take care of the rest. It will all unfold as you wish it to unfold. And I say this not to soothe you, but because it's the way it is. This is your reality, my friend; and I am only here to help you realize your dream of becoming the writer you always wanted to be. I have faith in you, and I will see you to the happy end. I promise."

"There's nothing I want more than to see Penny to a graceful retirement. That's what I wish for, Padre. Just to see us transition into a happy, graceful retirement. Is that possible?"

"It is, and it is in the process of happening as you wish it to be."

"I'm going to edit a few more chapters of *The Gnostic Way of Life,* and then I'm going to do some reading. Thank you for your comforting words."

"You're more than welcome, my friend...

49. Christmas Day: 2017

Monday, December 25, 2017

"Good morning, Padre. This must be a special day for you, but for some reason it does not have the spark of excitement that Penny and I would like it to have, and I wonder why. Could it be because of all the disruption in our life this past year? I know that we are adjusting to a new frequency, but good gosh it's taking a long time to find some balance. In any event, Padre; I just want to tell you that on the whole, things are not as bleak as I want to think they are. What a strange thing to say. Why must my thoughts be colored with darkness instead of light? Have I become a victim of my own shadow—again? I hope not!"

"No, you have not become a victim of your own shadow. These are the normal concerns of one's life, and you and your loved one have had a lot of concerns this past year; but I promise that your new year will be much more rewarding, and I say this not just to soothe your bruised emotions, but because it will be so."

"Let me run this by you right now before I forget. Yesterday while I was editing the proof copy of *My Writing Life* (my sequel to *The Lion that Swallowed Hemingway*), I got the strongest nudge— almost an imperative! —to take out my novel *The Gadfly* that I wrote more than twenty-five years ago and rework it, because now I can flesh it in and do it justice. As soon as I finish proofreading *My Writing Life*, I may just do that. What do you think?"

"I would say yes, but it is your decision. But remember, no decision is the right decision because all decisions are right for their own reasons. If you still feel this way when you finish proofing your new book, by all means do so; and I can assure you, that if you do it will demand your most creative efforts, because this novel will call upon your life as never before. It will be your most autobiographical novel, in a way that will be a marvel even to you."

"I'm tempted, Padre; I really am. Now, what's going on with my mouth and teeth? I'm afraid to even talk about this."

A Sign of Things to Come

"Get a dental appointment in the New Year. Everything will be fine. I promise."

"Thank you for the reassurance. I need it if I want to continue writing."

"You do need reassurance, and I am here for you."

"I'm going to go downstairs and put on a nice fire in our airtight wood stove so Penny can have a nice atmosphere to do her Christmas cooking, preparing the dressing and getting the turkey ready for dinner, and her baking (she doesn't know what kind of pie she's going to make yet, a choice between pumpkin, apple, and blueberry), and then I'm going to go outside and shovel the driveway because it snowed during the night, and it might snow again today but I want to get a jump on it. Penny's been doing the driveway so far, not wanting me to do it for fear I may get a heart attack; but heh, if I'm going to go, I'm going to go, and my only regret would be leaving Penny, who has become my whole life. I do so wish we can have a happy, graceful retirement, which we will never be able to do until we sell our triplex up north. Please, Padre..."

"Yes, it will sell in the New Year; and you and Penny will have the life you have dreamt of having. This is not a promise, it is a fact. I see it."

"I sure hope so. Okay, Padre; I have to go and light the fire and do the driveway. Thank you for the reassurance, and until we talk again."

"My love for you and your loved one this special day."

"Thank you..."

50. New Year's Day: 2018

Monday, January 1, 2018

"Good morning, Padre. I had a curious experience this morning when I turned on the stairwell lights to go downstairs to make our morning coffee, the light blew out, and I'd like to know if this was a sign of things to come. I interpreted it to mean that the light of the old year has gone out and when I change the bulb a new light will usher in. What do you think?'

"That's a valid interpretation."

"The new light of a higher frequency, I would hope."

"Certainly. You have resolved a lot of karma this past year, and now you can look forward to new beginnings. It's all good, my friend."

January 3, 2018...

"Sorry for not continuing our chat on New Year's Day, I got sidetracked and did not come back; but I'd like to take it from where we left off, which is the business of a new frequency. I'm not quite sure what that means. Can you explain it to me?"

"A new frequency means a new vibration. It could be higher or lower. In your case, it would be higher because of the karmic resolutions you had this past year. Which means that your life is going to flow differently. How differently remains to be seen."

"I'm being inundated with a flood of insignificance, and if I don't get out from under I think I'm going to get moody and depressed. What would you suggest I do?

"Read, write, read, write and do your daily chores."

"I'm tired, Padre. I'm tired of my life. I need an infusion of inspiration."

"Your reading will give you much inspiration. Read Paul and Me *(Paul Newman and A. E. Hotchner). That's a very inspiring story. As is* The Way of the Writer, *by Charles Johnson. Try to read all the*

books that Penny got you for Christmas. They will give you the inspiration you are looking for. Each author will speak to your new frequency."

"Okay, I will. I'll start right now, with *Paul and Me*. I'll read one chapter and then one chapter of *The Way of the Writer* and then finish the first chapter of Joyce Carol Oates's *Soul at the White Heat*. That should get the infusion of inspiration started. Oh, I should mention that I just finished writing what I think is a wonderful spiritual musing. It was inspired by a poem I wrote last week, 'The Eyes Behind Her Eyes.' What did you think of it? And I hope you don't mind my need for reassurance, because I do feel somewhat insignificant today."

"Not at all. It's an insightful poem which will give the reader their first glimpse of the shadow self. You did your muse proud, especially by following it up with a spiritual musing to explain how your poem got to be written. Now do your reading and get on with you day. It will unfold gracefully, and your life will synchronize with the new frequency that you have earned through your karmic resolutions. Have a nice day, my friend."

"Thank you for your understanding. I'm going to do my reading first, and then I'm going to shower and wash my hair. Until we talk again…

51. My Amazon Wish List Christmas Gift

Thursday, January 4, 2018

"Good morning, Padre. Well, I did start reading three of the books that were on my Amazon wish list that Penny gave me for Christmas (she got me twelve books this year); I browsed the books first, and then I read a chapter of each book while sipping my first cup of coffee. The three books that I chose were: *Paul and Me,* by A. E. Hotchner (who wrote my favorite Hemingway memoir, *Papa Hemingway*); *The Way of the Writer, Reflections on the Art and Craft of Storytelling,* by Charles Johnson; and *Soul at the White Heat, Inspiration, Obsession, and the Writing Life,* by Joyce Carol Oates. And this morning I read the next two chapters of Oates's book after proof reading several chapters of my own book *My Writing Life* and editing my new spiritual musing, 'The Eyes Behind Her Eyes.' And now I'd like to chat with you."

"By all means. And did your reading improve your mood?"

"Yes. I even put on a little fire in our airtight wood stove to give the house a nice cozy feel, which Penny appreciated when she got home from work. We sat and had a drink before dinner, which I had on the stove ready to go—gnocchi with meatballs and sausage and a side of cauliflower with oil and balsamic vinegar dressing, all in all a very nice dinner; so thank you for inspiring me to read and set my day right."

"You're welcome. Reading is your way out of the humdrum of daily life routines. It's also what you need to feed your mind. Your mind needs information, and reading is the best way to get it. Not TV. TV is good for some information, but reading is much more rewarding for you. It keeps your mind active because you have to think while you are reading. Watching TV is more passive and less effective for feeding your mind. So, make a habit of reading more. Try to read all the books that Penny got you for Christmas. This will do you more good than you realize."

A Sign of Things to Come

"I'll try. Let me list the books that Penny gave me for Christmas this year. Aside from the three books already mentioned, she gave me *How to Read and Why,* by Harold Bloom; *Desperate Characters*, a novel by Paula Fox; *If on a winter's night a traveler,* a novel by Italo Calvino; *Lovely, Dark, Deep*, a book of short stories by Joyce Carol Oates; *The Idiot,* a novel by Fyodor Dostoevsky; *Ten Windows, How Great Poems Transform the World,* by Jane Hirshfield; *Great Short Works of Fyodor Dostoevsky*; and finally, *The Kybalion, A Study of the Hermetic Philosophy of Ancient Egypt and Greece*, by Three Hermits. I also got two more books from Penny's sister that were also on my Amazon wish list: *The Broken Tower, The Life of Hart Crane,* by Paul Mariani, and *The Essential Jung*, Selected and Introduced by Anthony Storr. These books came in before Christmas and I started reading them right away. But I also received another book that was Penny's gift to me. This one came in a few days after Christmas, shipped on its own: *Letters of Emily Dickinson*, Edited by Mabel Loomis Todd. I started reading this one, but it's not as engaging as I thought it would be. Maybe it will pull me in because I love Dickinson's poetry. I was hoping she'd be a little more revealing in her letters, but not yet. So, I've got a lot of nice reading ahead of me. And it's time I read some stories and novels. I need this kind of reading, which I keep putting off for other genres. What do you think, Padre?"

"I think you're right. You need to read more fiction. This is going to help you in your own creative writing. Start with Joyce Carol Oates's book of short stories."

"Why?"

"She is an excellent writer with a special talent for creating stories. She has a gift that will rub off on you. Trust me. Read her book of stories first."

"Straight through, or in conjunction with other books?"

"If at all possible, straight through; or two or three stories at a time."

"What about Dostoevsky?"

"He's a special case. Read him for the gravity of life. He will give you what you need for your own stories. He will give you a way to delve deeper into your characters. Joyce will give you the freedom to let your imagination soar. Both will help you considerably."

"I wish I could be as motivated to write my own fiction as I am to write books on my own life's journey of self-discovery. I've only got a few more chapters to go to finish my book *The Gnostic Way of Life,* which I've put off for the past week; but maybe reading these new books will help combust my imagination for my creative writing. What do you think?

"It will. This is why I suggest you read Oates's book of stories, and then Dostoevsky along with the other books you have started reading."

"I think I'm going to put on pizza dough today. I'm also going to put on another fire and read in the cozy atmosphere of our sun room. Thank you, Padre. We'll chat again when the spirit moves me."

"By all means. Have a nice reading day, my friend."

"Oh! I forgot to ask you about *The Kybalion,* the book on Hermetic wisdom. Where do you stand on this book?"

"This book will give you new words and concepts to expand upon your own philosophy of life. It will add to your understanding of the way. It will not surprise you much, because you have been initiated into the deepest mystery of the way, which is the gnostic way of your own life; so, it is worth reading. The benefit of this book is that it will confirm your own understanding of the way, which will boost your self-confidence considerably. It was a good choice for your wish list."

"On that note, until we chat again…"

52. The Thin Edge of the Wedge

Friday, January 12, 1018

"Good morning, Padre. I have to run something by you. It's of growing importance, and I suspect it may be the subject of a new spiritual musing, and quite possibly one of the closing chapters of my narrative essay *The Gnostic Way of Life*, but I'd like to run it by you first to see if we can dig out the creative premise of this new insight which I am simply calling 'the thin edge of the wedge' because in this insight I see social consciousness being pried apart by a new paradigm of belief that may be exactly what the world needs to lift it up to a new moral awareness so the world can keep from sliding in the bowels of its own nothingness. Are you up to a little discourse on this new insight? Or am I a little ahead of my time here?"

"Not at all. In fact, you are in absolute sync with the spiritual consciousness of the future, which is why you have seen it as the thin edge of the wedge. This new spiritual consciousness is going to change the paradigm of the world's thinking, and you are absolutely correct in your understanding that the new morality will come out of this new paradigm; but it will be a slow process, taking dozens of years before it even begins to sprout. But all seeds have to begin their growth in time, and they have now been sown and will soon sprout. You will help them to sprout with your writing. Now you can see how relevant your writing will be to this evolving new morality that the world is about to give birth to. Yes, you did come upon the gifted psychic medium channel to expand your own horizons, and in your research of the Afterlife Interviews *on the* Shiny Show *you began to realize just how the new morality was taking form. Now I believe you would like to talk about your current timeline with respect to your old timeline, or your parallel lives; your lifetime as Orest Stocco who did not achieve what he was contracted to achieve, and your parallel current lifetime in which you fulfilled your contract and realized your true self?"*

"That's what I'd like to talk about. I'd like to know if my two lives have been interlaced, because I cannot make heads or tails of my dreams in which I am myself but not myself, I am with old acquaintances, but my life does not seem the same. What's going on, Padre?"

"This is the mystery of the redemptive principle of life. You have merged your two lives because you are one true self now in your identity as Orest Stocco. You managed to make your being and non-being into one identity, and as Orest Stocco you no longer exist as the shadow-conflicted self that you were in your first life as Orest Stocco. This is why your dreams are so hard to explain. They are dreams of your two selves but with one identity, and your behavior in your dreams reflects both aspects of yourself in your new realized identity. It's no wonder that you are confused. But soon you will be having dreams of just one self, your current identity in its wholeness and completeness as Orest Stocco."

"Am I on the mark with my concept of the thin edge of the wedge?"

"More than you realize. Explore it in your spiritual musing first, because this genre will be more revealing than if you try to work it out in your chapter for your book."

"I think I will, but I don't think just quite yet. I feel I have to watch a few more *Shiny Shows* with Kari and Alison before I can write my spiritual musing."

"A few more afterlife interviews and you will be ready. You will be so confident in your perspective that it will come through naturally in your spiritual musing. Trust your muse."

"So, can I ask you now? Are you my higher self?"

"You know the answer to that."

"Yes and no."

"Correct."

"That's the conclusion that Jung came to, wasn't it? He realized that the Self was Philemon, and he was the evolving Self; right?"

"Correct."

"And these chats we're having, they're an exercise in facilitating my higher self?"

"You could put it like that."

"Tell me, Padre; now that I have already seen all of those afterlife interviews with famous and not-so-famous people, I've come to see that life continues on the other side with the same consciousness that one crosses over with, which means that one must continue to grow and evolve over there in the path that they have taken, or begin a new path; which?"

"Either. They have lived their life and have died, which means that they have either fulfilled their spiritual contract or not, and it's up to them to continue their life. As you have seen, most seem to continue with their same life; but those that have fulfilled their contract are ready to move onto another path to their higher self. This is the journey of the self."

"So, what I'm exploring in my writing—the gnostic way of life—would be as relevant over there as it is down here?"

"Absolutely."

"The veil has parted for me then—or, I have confirmed the transparency of the evolving self on both sides of the great divide, and it makes no difference to my writing because life is a journey of the self?

"Absolutely correct."

"I just got a flash of an insight that I will be imbuing my novel *The Gadfly* with this new awareness. My protagonist David Oakly will be awake to both sides of the great divide. Am I going to be rewriting this novel with this new awareness?"

"You said that you wanted a new burst of inspiration. Well, you just got it. With this new premise your old novel will become a novel for the new paradigm. It will be your literary equivalent of The Shiny Show and Afterlife Interviews. *David Oakly is the man of the future, the whole man who speaks for the emerging new morality. This is your creative challenge, my friend."*

"Can you give me an infusion of creative energy so I can get this started. I have a few more chapters to write for *The Gnostic Way of Life*, so when can I expect to start work on my novel *The Gadfly*? I'd like to get it started as soon as possible."

"Once you have done your research on the emerging new paradigm and written your spiritual musing on the thin edge of the wedge, then you will take out your manuscript and open up a new file and begin reworking your novel from your new perspective. I can tell you right now that your protagonist David Oakly will be a character

to be remembered. He will be your literary Zarathustra, and he will take the literary world by storm. This I can promise you."

"I can see it happening. David Oakly will be whole and complete within the literary framework of my ideal self; correct?"

"He will be the ideal of the new paradigm. The Self of the individuation process."

"I don't feel like exploring this any further, because if I do I will be taking away some of that magical dust off the butterfly's wings."

"You will. So, why don't we wrap it up for today?"

"One more question. Any surprises for me down the road? You know, those little surprises that throw my world out of whack?"

"No more surprises. Get to work. You have to get your book finished and your new spiritual musing written. We'll talk again soon."

"Thanks, Padre."

"You're welcome…"

53. An Idea for a New Book

Monday, February 5, 2018

"Good morning, Padre. It's been a while. I've been meaning to call on you, but for one reason or another I kept putting it off. Today I'd like to reconnect. I have some things I have to get off my mind. One thing is this tense jaw issue that I seem to have developed. It's because of my teeth, and I still refuse to make a dental appointment. If I don't do something soon I'm going to start hating myself, and that won't be any fun. I've written some new spiritual musings and have been posting them on my blog, one every Saturday; but I don't get much response. I do love writing them, though. They help clear up a lot of personal issues. I'm still working on my new book, *The Gnostic Way of Life*, but I'm getting tired of that and hope to bring it home as soon as possible so I can move on to another project. And speaking of new projects, the idea for a book not unlike *Tuesday's with Morrie* by Mitch Albom has begun to take hold of me. Mine would be called *Sundays with Sharon*. It would be based upon my Sunday morning tea with a woman who has become an ardent reader of my books. I have called her Sharon. What do you think of this project? Is it worth pursuing?"

"As always, when an idea comes to you for a new book you can rest assured that the idea came from your higher self, and you would not have received it were it not part of your destined purpose. Of course, I agree. It will make an excellent book, with or without Sharon's active participation. Trust your judgment and do what you must."

"Actually, I was thinking of starting the first chapter this morning after Penny goes to work. I had tea with Sharon yesterday morning (*Sunday, February 4, 2018*) and we talked about the spiritual musing I had posted the day before and the book I had brought for her to read. I brought *Tuesday's with Morrie* for her to read because I wanted to plant the seed for my own book *Sundays with Sharon*. I didn't share with her my idea for my book which would be based upon our Sunday morning talks, I just wanted to plant the seed and see what became of it. But she's not stupid, and I'm sure she'll figure it out. What do you think?"

"She hasn't made the connection yet, but she will. Start your book this morning and let your muse guide you. This book will give you new inspiration and will be good for you."

"I really would like her participation. I would like to tape our conversations, but I have to wait and see before I ask her. It would be a big commitment for her."

"It would. But she would also see the opportunity for her own growth, which you should stress when you ask her to actively participate in your project."

"I should ask her higher self first, shouldn't I?"

"That would be the appropriate way to go."

"And so, I shall. Right now, in fact. Give me a moment, Please…. I call upon my friend's higher self and ask for permission to tape our Sunday morning conversations for a book I have planned, which is to be called *Sunday's with Sharon*. Do I have your permission to ask her?"

"…Sharon's higher self speaking. This is a big commitment for her, but she is willing to go along with it as long as you keep it strictly between the two of you. She does not want to involve her family, if at all possible."

"I suspected that, but I'm sure that in the course of our conversations she won't be able to keep her family out of our conversations. That's just how conversations are."

"I know. You have my blessing. Ask and she will agree."

"Then I'm asking you now. Can you plant the seed for her to be aware of my intentions?"

"I will."

"Thank you. Now I'd like to continue my talk with Padre Pio…Padre, I just got permission from Sharon's higher self, so I'll just have to wait and see what happens."

"As I said, start your project this morning and see what happens."

"Now, about all this other stuff going on in my life. I don't know what to make of it. I seem to be shifting to a new perspective and I'm in state of mild confusion. Can you tell me what's going on?

A Sign of Things to Come

Am I on the cusp of what I perceive to be a new spiritual awakening?"

You most certainly are. This is where your confusion comes in. You have been awakened to this new spiritual awakening with your research on spirit channeling. You have opened up to the other side and your third eye will be opening more each day. Just go about your daily life doing what you normally do and just let it happen. Keep focussed on your writing. You need that focus to keep your mind occupied while you adjust to the new awakening."

"I will. Thank you, Padre."

"You're welcome..."

54. A Big Thank You

Tuesday, March 20, 2018

"Thank you, Padre. Thank you for the sale of our triplex. Penny told me that she wrote you a letter asking for your help to sell our triplex up north, and we received the documents of the sale yesterday, and all we have to do is sign them and then have our lawyer work out the details. We still have a mortgage on the triplex, which I believe is around thirty thousand dollars; but by the time we pay off all our mortgage and bills, I believe Penny and I will have a nice little sum to put away to ensure us some small measure of economic comfort. So, thank you again, Padre; I know you had a hand in this, and I thank you especially for Penny's sake."

"You're welcome, my friend. It's been a long time coming, but now you and your loved one can live your life free of the anxiety of having to run your triplex from so far away. It will be a good home for the buyer, and he will appreciate it the way you would like. And to answer your unasked question, there will be no surprises in finalizing the deal."

"I was surprised that Penny wrote you a letter, but I think you wanted to make a believer out of her, and you have. As soon as this deal finalizes with the money in our account, she will be one happy woman. As for myself, I'm still processing the whole thing and won't come to terms with it until I do. It has been one long, long journey for me, building this triplex and all that it entailed; and I would like to write a story on this someday. And speaking of writing, I didn't finish writing *The Gnostic Way of Life* yet (I have three or four more chapters to write) because I was called to writing a novel memoir called *Sundays with Sharon*, and it's taking me to new horizons of perception. What do you think of this project?"

"This book will be one of your best, capturing readers from the first page. It will take the reader to where all of your other books have taken them, but only with more poignancy and meaning. I cannot tell you how proud I am of this book. It is the culmination of your writing, and I am enjoying how it is unfolding."

A Sign of Things to Come

"Alright, let's get to my health. My teeth. What the hell is going on?"

"You have to get to a dentist so you can rid yourself of the self-embarrassment. Do not worry about your teeth. They will be fixed and you will get your smile back. Take care of your finances with the sale of your triplex and everything will fall into place. I promise you."

"Thank you. I needed to hear that."

"You're welcome."

55. The Deal's Almost Closed

Tuesday, April 24, 2018

"Good afternoon, Padre. I've been meaning to talk with you for a while now, but I've been putting it off. I'm anxious about the closing of the sale of our triplex, which is to be completed May 15th, I think. I'm beset with little demons of apprehension, which I've asked you several times (perhaps too many) to get rid of for me, and now we find out we have to replace the patio door on the middle apartment and I've asked you to smooth this over. I know we have to do it before the new owner takes over, but we have to find someone to do it; could you take care of that for us?"

"It's already taken care of. Don't worry, there are no surprises waiting for you. All is going well and you and Penny will get your graceful retirement. I promise you."

"Can I take that to the bank?"

"By all means."

"Okay. Now, about the two books I'm writing. I've put *Sundays with Sharon* on hold while I work on *One Rule to Live By: Be Good*, and I'd like to run some thoughts by you about both books. Let's start with the latter. The thought came to me to post this as a work in progress on my blog, one chapter at a time. What do you think?"

"It will draw you into the public arena and it will expose your books to the public, and it will go a long way to launching your career. It will be an exciting journey, and you will attract some attention; but on the whole, your writing will not be for everybody. You will have a following that will be financially rewarding; so, yes, go ahead and do it. I will be there for you when you need me. All will be well, I assure you."

"Do you think I've taken liberties with Jordan Peterson?"

"He's in the public domain. His books and thoughts are out there, and you are responding to his books and thoughts. No, you

haven't taken liberties with him. You are entering a discourse on his books and thoughts."

"What about him personally? Will he respond?"

"Not immediately. He will have to think about your writing. It's still too much for him to process, despite his great capacity for thinking."

"What do you think of the book *One Rule to Live By: Be Good*?"

"It needs to be written, and you are the only one who can write it. It brings Jordan Peterson's thought process to the secret way where you are writing from. He's almost there, and he needs that extra push. You book will do that for him. He will follow your chapters on your spiritual musings blog, but he will not respond. He will be a watchful observer."

"I was thinking of posting the first chapter this Saturday."

"Wait one more week. Next Saturday will be more in keeping with the natural forces of your life. They will be aligned properly for the public release of your work in progress. It will be a very interesting book to follow, and many will—many, many, and many!"

"I'll believe it when I see it."

"You will see it, and you will believe it. And I will be there to enjoy it with you."

"Okay, Padre; now the big question: are we going to get together this summer for the sequel to *Healing with Padre Pio*?"

"That is purely up to you. I've been waiting for you. You will be financially free to do so, and I expect you will. So, let's make a date and go for it."

"You choose the date, then."

"How about we start some time in June, or early July?"

"That sounds fine with me. Okay, Padre; make this happen."

"With your permission."

"You have it. Now, how will the public respond to *One Rule to Live By?* It does go beyond the material perspective on life and introduces the spiritual dimension. Is the public ready?"

"Not only ready but waiting impatiently."

"You're kidding?"

"Seeing is believing. Wait and see. I promise, the public is waiting."

"Why am I so apprehensive?"

"It's many things. Your teeth, closing the deal on your house, your book with Sharon, your apprehension of going public with your thoughts on Peterson; many things. But all is well, my friend. You have come too far to frustrate yourself. By the end of June your life will be where you and Penny have dreamed of it being. Again, I promise you. Now, get on with your day and don't fret about anything. Everything is taken care of. Ciao for now and have a wonderful afternoon. And read and write and write and write and write. Writing is your source of energy and your grace and power. Write write write!"

"Thank you."

"You're welcome...."

"I'm back, Padre. It's a little after 8 P.M. and I'd like to run something by you. I've been watching some Peterson interviews and I'm getting intimidated enough to question my confidence in the book I'm writing, *One Rule to Live By: Be Good*. This isn't good, is it? If I can be cute about it."

"You can be cute about it, and it isn't good for you to question your own confidence, so don't do it. Just write what you are inspired to write, as you always do, because your inspiration is your gift. It is not your mind. Jordan Peterson has a brilliant mind. That is his gift. You are not on the same mental plane as he is. You are on the spiritual plane with your insights. He's on the mental plane with his thoughts. He has gone as far as the mind can take him. This is why he has taken the world by storm. He's looking down on the world from the great heights of the mind, and he's making a lot of sense. He's giving everyone something to think about. Your book is taking you to the furthest reaches of the soul plane where soul and God are one. You cannot compare your thinking with his. His thinking is deductive and far reaching, but you've been down that road with Pythagoras and you had to move on. You had to abandon the ways of the mind, so to speak, to find the ways of spirit, or the way of Soul. You did. Don't compare yourself with him and don't question your confidence. Write from your heart, not your mind."

"I fear putting myself to the test, if you know what I mean?"

A Sign of Things to Come

"I know exactly what you mean, and you need not fear. When you are put in a position of speaking about your writing you will do much better than you think. You will speak from your own experiences and your own truth. You cannot speak from any other place."

"But will it be enough?"

"More than enough. I assure you."

"Have I misjudged my connection with Jordan Peterson?"

"No. He's aware of your books. He's even read them, not completely because he's much too busy to sit down and read them right through; but they intrigue him, and he's made a point of reading them through without interruption. He will do so when he's called."

"And have I gone too far writing my book *One Rule to Live By: Be Good?*"

"No. Your book is a creative exploration of the idea that inspired the book, the idea that Jordan Peterson is answering the question of your poem. It is a wonderful idea to explore. It gets you exposed to what's going on in the world and giving you new reading material. Your book is going to evolve into much more than what it is. Trust your muse."

"What is the world's fascination with Jordan Peterson?"

"You have the answer, which you are exploring in your book. He is the hierophant the world has been waiting for. Take that theme and go with it."

"What's the simplest, most effective advice you can give on writing this book?"

"Write from the heart. Let your heart guide you. Listen to your oracle. Today's experience with the lady who cut your hair is a good example of how your oracle is guiding you. Make that part of your book. Use it to explain how inarticulate young people are. Make the mentoring of these young people the missing factor of their life. The simplest advice that I can give you is to write from your heart. Feel what you are writing. Feel it from the bottom of your heart. Make every word count. Trust your oracle. It's who you are. It's your superior self."

"One more thing. Thank you for getting us someone to do the patio door on our triplex. I hope it goes well, and I hope the deal closes without a hitch."

"You and Penny have nothing to worry about. Very soon you will have the life you want and dreamt of having. Now give yourself a break and stop fretting. We can chat again when you have had a good sleep."

"Why don't you visit me in my dreams?"

"I will. Go to sleep with me on your mind and I will visit you."

"I will. Thank you for this."

"You're welcome..."

56. The Deal Has Closed

Thursday, May 24, 2018

"Thank you, Padre. The deal has closed. It's been nine days since it closed and Penny and I are still not quite adjusted to our new reality. The anxiety of our triplex is no longer with us, and it will take time for the memory of all that anxiety to leave us. But I want to say thank you again for what you did for us, and I know you went out of your way to make our sale happen. I had no idea that Penny had written you a letter asking for your help, but I'm glad she did. Now we are adjusting and getting on with our life. The next thing I have to take care of is my teeth. I'm afraid to go to the dentist, and I ask again for your help. But I am happy to say that my book *One Rule to Live By: Be Good* is going better than I expected. I'm on Chapter 23. I was going to get into it this morning, but I have house duties to attend to. Again, Padre; thank you."

"You're welcome, my friend. I'm very happy for you and Penny. Yes, she did write me a letter, and it was very moving. The lessons you both had to learn are now complete. You paid your dues to your community and are now free to move in new directions. You both no longer have that psychic burden to carry. You are free to live your life in happy anticipation."

"What do you think of my book so far?"

"It has taken even me by surprise. It is flowing smoothly and much better than I expected. I cannot wait to see how your oracle brings it to resolution. It has a way to go yet, and you will not complete it until you read Peterson's other book, Maps of Meaning; *and then you will bring it to closure. Yes, we will arrange this summer for our next project together. And your teeth will be taken care of. I promise you, no surprises. Just make the appointment and get started. It will take a few appointments, but you will get them in order. Trust me, my friend; all will be well."*

"I don't know what to say, Padre. I think I'm going to shave and brush my teeth and then I'm going to go out and cut up those limbs that I cut down from our dead tree, and maybe get our burn barrel going to clean up some of that brush. And I'm putting on a spaghetti sauce for dinner. Our lawn tractor won't start, and it is leaking gas. Penny and I will look at when she comes home from work. She's going to get some information from Canadian Tire. I hope we get to work out a schedule for our next project this summer, which will go into the winter; and I hope that I get some followers on my blog for the book I'm posting. This Saturday I'll be posting my fourth chapter. Any advice on how to promote it?"

"Facebook and Twitter for now. You will snag interest in the next few weeks. I can't tell you yet. Just keep on doing what you are doing. Now get on with your day. We'll talk again when you have calmed down. You need to go out and do some work to level yourself off. Okay, my friend; have a wonderful day."

"*Ciao* for now, then…

57. Looking for Focus

Tuesday, May 30, 2018

"I'm here, Padre; but I'm not here. I don't know where I am. Can you tell me where I am? I would like to know how to refocus myself. I feel lost in a world of my own unknowing. What do I have to do to get back into focus? Our lawn tractor is out of commission. We lost the little rubber stopper (I don't know what else to call it) for the carburetor and Anthony, the serviceman, has to get a new one someplace, which means our lawn tractor won't be fixed until he gets it; and today I'm going to book a dentist appointment and I dread going. What's going on with my life now that our triplex has sold? I feel like I'm floating and waiting to land. Or I've landed and with a thump. What's going on with me?"

"Why don't you go and have your shower and then we can talk?"

"I will. Talk to you in a few minutes…"

"Are you feeling a little better now?"
"Yes."
"What were your thoughts as you showered?"

"I thought that life is basically what it is, and that I'm concentrating on aspects of life that are in somewhat of a turmoil. I've been doing a lot of video watching on the Jordan Peterson phenomenon, and I'm a little off my center. Is that what's wrong?"

"That and your anxiety about going to the dentist. But I tell you my friend, there is no need to be anxious. It is all routine for the dentist. She will get your teeth done and you will go on with your life in what you have to do to complete your mission. What else did you think about while showering?"

"The thought came to me that I had picked up some of my serviceman's energy and that I felt down and heavy because of it."

"You did. But he picked up some of your energy and feels better. You did him a service, and you will be rewarded for that. Now what else came to your mind?"

"That to focus my mind I should read some essays."

"Then do so. Once you get your mind back in focus you will be okay. Don't worry about your dentist appointment. Again, I promise everything will be okay. Now get on with your day and don't get too far removed from your book. Get back into it tomorrow. Your story is going where it needs to go, and you are going to finish it by the end of the year. You have to read Peterson's Maps of Meaning *first, so order it as soon as possible."*

"It seems that my last posting of my book on my blog did not attract much attention. I feel my writing is much too deep for the readers to consider."

"Don't worry about that. Just keep writing your book. It will find its readers. This I can assure you, because your book speaks to the deeper levels of the soul, and the soul needs this nourishment badly. You are on the right course. Just keep writing."

"I will. Anything else I need to know?"

"You're good to go, my friend."

"Thank you, Padre."

"You're welcome…"

58. Second Dentist Appointment

Wednesday, July 4, 2018

"Good morning, Padre. I'm going downstairs to get a cup of coffee, and then we can chat for a while; please wait a moment or two…Okay, I'm back. It's been a little over a month since we last talked, and as much as I dreaded going, I did go to the dentist, and she did do one cavity, and today she's going to work on the tooth that chipped, but we don't know if it will hold, so I got a price for a crown (two grand) if and when it has to be done, and next week I have to go for another appointment to extract the tooth that cracked because it can't be fixed, and then I will look into getting a plate for my bottom teeth (another couple of grand, if not more), which means I'll have to put off getting the implant I wanted for my top missing tooth. Wow! So, tell me, Padre; have I been humbled enough yet, or have I still more humbling to endure?"

"Good morning, my friend. It's good to be talking again. You need to get this out of your system, so please continue our conversations. They keep you connected to your inspiration, and you need the best connection possible for your writing. To answer your question first; yes, you will be experiencing more humbling, because life, as you say, is a journey through vanity to humility, and humility will never be realized in one lifetime. As you know from our book Healing with Padre Pio*, I did not experience my humility until I crossed over; that's when my vanity finally left me, and I experienced the glory of being my true self unencumbered by ego. But don't put too much emphasis on this, because you have worked your way through the bedrock of your vanity and are only cleaning up the residual effects of your ego self. Your teeth will be fine, and you will get on with your life. I assure you."*

"Well, we've gone through another long weekend without the dreaded phone call from one of our tenants, and Penny and I are just getting used to being triplex-anxiety free; so, thank you Padre for getting our triplex sold. And now we're going to be spending some of our money on an air conditioner. Penny cannot stand the heat wave we've been experiencing, and she threatened to go up north if we didn't get an air conditioner; so yesterday we got a price and tomorrow he's coming to install it. Hope all goes well. Now, my new book, *One Rule to Live By: Be Good,* I've put it on hold for the summer. I got two thirds of it written, but I have to do a lot of reading this summer before I finish it; so, I'm on hiatus. What do you think of it so far?"

"I like it. It's much better than I expected it to be. Not that I didn't have faith in you, but we never know how the creative spirit works its magic. The creative process is the central mystery of man's nature, and it doesn't matter how evolved a soul becomes, the creative spirit will always surprise us. That's the mystery of divinity. You will get the bulk of your reading done this summer, and you will complete your book before Christmas, and then you will complete your book Sundays with Sharon, *and this will make you ready for our sequel to* Healing with Padre Pio *in the spring, which will take all of next summer and fall to complete. Just before Christmas you will have it all done and ready to publish. I'm looking forward to it."*

"So, we won't start it this summer, then?"

"It doesn't look like it. It was in the cards, but you got too involved with your new book and that's more important. You have to see your creative process through. When your oracle calls, you have to listen; that's what keeps the channels open."

"I read a few chapters (skimmed, that is) of *Healing with Padre Pio* the other day, I had to look up something you said to me, about me providing a new way of thinking, a new way of perceiving, a new way of understanding with my writing, and I couldn't get over how the book read; it felt like someone else had written it. God, was I in the zone when I wrote it!"

"You were. And you will be again with the sequel."

"I hope so, because that's a great place to be. Anyway, about this new way of thinking, perceiving, and understanding; should I capitalize on it and just write my books, with no apologies or explanations for my point of view?"

"Yes. Your writing will be refreshing. Just keep doing what you are doing."

A Sign of Things to Come

"I will. Now I have to share something with you. I have never felt so good since we sold our triplex, because Penny and I are finally beginning to experience what we've been waiting to experience for a long time, a graceful retirement. We're not quite there yet because Penny is still working, but good God it's nice to be in our little corner of joyful plenitude, as I expressed our new state of consciousness since we sold our triplex. Again, thank you Padre."

"And it can only get better."

"So, this summer I have a ton of reading to do—Tolstoy, Dostoevsky, Solzhenitsyn, and Peterson's *Maps of Meaning*, plus some Nietzsche—and speaking of Nietzsche, I have to ask you something. I think he threw a monkey wrench into the system. He was crazy, brilliant but crazy all the same. I believe it. He went crazy trying to reconcile his being and non-being, and he gave the world such a heavy dose of nihilism—justification for it, that is—that the world has never recovered from his philosophy. I think he did the world a great disfavor. He made atheism popular. I don't know how else to express my feelings about him, but I have the gut feeling that the world would have been a much better place without his philosophical inquiry."

"If not him, someone else would have come along because that's how life is supposed to work, from the world of being to the world of non-being and back again, the two extremes of the evolutionary dynamic have to be played out; it's hard-wired to work that way. But you are right to feel the way you do about Nietzsche. I could never make sense of him when I learned about his philosophy. But you have to read him for your own book, so read a few of his books and get the feel of the man; that way your book will have the depth of gravitas it needs to give it all the credibility it must have to carry the message your oracle wishes to convey."

"Here's a question about my book, then. Given Jordan Peterson's rise in popularity, can my book catch the wave he's riding since my book was inspired by his book *12 Rules for Life: An Antidote to Chaos*? My book takes over where his book leaves off. Am I right in this?"

"Yes. Your book opens the door that his book takes one to. And yes, your book will catch the wave he's riding, and it will cause some to rethink their life. Your book was called for, and it will serve

the purpose it was called to serve. That, I assure you, will happen. And, I'm happy to tell you, it will happen in your lifetime, and it will add that extra dimension to your life that you and your loved one so richly deserve. It will fill your little corner of joyful plenitude with all the freedom and mobility that you and Penny have been working for. Don't think about it, though; just do what you have to do, and let God do the rest."

"What about my twin soul book to this one, *Sunday's with Sharon*? Am I right in twining these two books?"

"They were meant to be born together like your other twin soul books, Death, the Final Frontier *and* The Merciful Law of Divine Synchronicity. *This new set of twins have their own message, a message that will become clear to you when you complete both books."*

"About the ultimate purpose of life?"

"In a sense, yes. They will open the door to the big mystery of life, and that's why you were called to write them."

"Padre, I'm getting exhausted, creatively speaking. Thank you for this talk. I'm going to try to keep our channel open. Until we talk again, then."

"Ciao, my friend. And don't worry, your dental appointments will all go well, and you will be free of that anxiety by the end of the month. Then you can concentrate on getting your summer duties done and be ready to finish your book."

"Until the next time, then…"

59. The Extraction

"Good morning, Padre. I just showered, and I'm going downstairs to get a cup of coffee; and then we can chat, if you don't mind."

"Of course not. Get your coffee and we can talk about what's on your mind…"

"I've got my coffee, and as I was walking up the stairs it occurred to me to tell you about Penny's quilt. She just finished it yesterday, and she's really proud of it. She went over to our neighbors because Joni wanted to see it when it was finished, and they loved it. Penny came back very proud of herself. And she should be. She's very happy doing what she loves to do. Doing is her path, and when she's doing she's the happiest. This is your teaching, isn't it?"

"Yes. Doing is the way to grow and understand. The more you do, the more you grow and understand. This is why I emphasis that you write and write and write. Writing is your doing, so don't worry about your Jordan Peterson book. You are doing what you were called to do, and in doing this book you are growing in ways you didn't think possible. Just keep writing it. You will get back into it later in the summer and it will flow to its resolution. I promise you will be happy with the result, and so will your readers."

"I was getting pretty worried yesterday. I felt like my confidence was being shaken, and it didn't feel good at all. I suddenly realized how outside the box I really am, and I doubted myself like never before. What was that about, anyway?"

"You were overwhelmed by all the videos you were watching. The state of consciousness of the people you watched on the subject of Jordan Peterson pulled you into the world of the politically confused, and the confusion got to you. Don't get too caught up in these videos. Watch a few at a time, but no more. Let your mind sift through the material and trust your creative self to do the rest. Just do your reading and ready yourself to complete your book."

"I've got a dentist appointment today. I'm going to have a tooth extracted. It cracked and can't be saved. I hope the extraction goes well. This leads to the possibility of getting a plate for my bottom teeth. I don't want to ask you about that because I don't' want to know."

"Your extraction will go well, and you will look into a plate. We can talk about this another time, but I will tell you it will go well."

My right leg is healing. I pulled a muscle a couple of weeks ago, and on the day that the servicemen installed our air conditioner I pulled my muscle some more when I lifted a patio stone to put into the wheelbarrow, and for a whole week I had to put Voltaren Extra Strength topical rub on my leg and wore a knee brace, which really helped. Now I'm beginning to walk normally again. It's not quite healed, but it's a lot better than what it was. It was painful. But I have to ask you something, if I may. I related my loss of physical mobility to karma. I think I got a karmic whiplash because of my vitriolic anger at my neighbor who put her house up for sale. I was vicious in my anger, because I saw the sale of her cottage as odious greed. She bought it two years ago for two hundred and ninety-seven thousand, and she put it up for sale for four hundred and fifty-nine thousand, and that kind of greed really got to me. I know this speaks to some deep-seated resentment, but I didn't care, and I cursed the woman for her greed. And then I got the leg thing and couldn't walk without pain. I inhibited her "mobility" by cursing her greed, and I got a karmic whiplash and inhibited my "mobility." Am I correct in my discernment?"

"A very good analysis. Yes, you paid for your curses. A good lesson for you, which you will write about more deeply in your book Sundays with Sharon. *A very good chapter it will make, too. This is your life, my friend. You do learn the hard way, don't you?"*

"Apparently so. Okay, now I want to get deep. I need some answers on this question. I can't help but feel that I am a man apart. I do not fit in with life. I feel so far removed from life that I don't know what to do. My writing is so far removed from the flow of social consciousness that I wonder what the hell I am doing posting my chapters on my blog. Is it all a waste of time?"

"What is your favorite expression?"

"Life is an individual journey."

A Sign of Things to Come

"Then just live your life and let God take care of the rest."

"That's putting a lot of trust in God, isn't it?"

"Now you're getting closer to what your writing is intended to do. Your purpose as a writer is to show the way, to help one realize the way, and to do that you have to tell your own journey to wholeness and completeness. Tell your stories and let God do the rest."

"May I ask you to go ahead of me this morning to the dentist office and let the aura of your love and compassion fill the place. I'd like that very much. I can't explain myself, but I know that your presence—whichever fragrance you wish to imbue the place with—will alleviate not only my anxiety, but the anxiety of everyone else. Can you do that for me, please?"

"Yes. I will imbue the place with an aura of peace. Harmony is the order of the day. Do not worry about your off-handed remark to your dentist. You will make up for it today."

"How?"

"It will come to you."

"Oh, I forgot to tell you. My dentist, Dr. Christina, did a miraculous job on my chipped tooth. She rebuilt it and I don't need a crown. At least, not yet. I hope it lasts."

"Yes, she did a wonderful job. Tell her again."

"About my reading. I'm reading the Russians. God, the existential anxiety that these people lived under. What the hell happened over there, anyway?"

"That's why you were called to write your new book. You were meant to open that door and become aware of the circumstances that led to that reality. In your awareness, you open the door for your reader to become aware. It is what you've been preparing for. You've made your journey to your true self, now you have to share your story with the world."

"This is getting me deeper and deeper into the shadow side of life. I can't help but feel that I'm going to be exploring the consciousness of nothingness (the Archetypal Shadow) in this last part of my book *One Rule to Live By: Be Good.*"

"Yes. This is where your book is headed. To be good is what life leads one to, because this virtue undermines the consciousness of

nothingness. It is a much bigger theme than you realize, but it will open up to you once you've done all your reading."

"Okay. I think we've covered all I needed to cover this morning."

"Yes. Don't worry about your appointment. It will go better than you think. I am always with you, my friend. Life will get better and better for you and your loved one. I promise."

"I love it when you assure me like that. Thank you, Padre."

"You're welcome..."

60. My Dental Appointment Went Well

Saturday, July 14, 2018

"Good morning, Padre. My dental appointment went well, but not what I expected; my blood pressure was too high for an extraction (204 over something; I can't remember what; but I had forgotten to take my heart medication in the morning), and Dr. Christina opted to do two fillings side by side instead, and she did an excellent job and built up my self-image again so I can smile without being self-conscious. I have another appointment on Monday, a cleaning; and the following Thursday I'll have the extraction. The curious thing is that after Dr. Cristina did my fillings, I asked to have my blood pressure taken again just to see what it would be, and it went down twenty points. Go figure!"

"You are correct in your observation that you are going to extract your phobia for dental work with your extraction, and your appointment last Thursday proves it; it was the start of your new attitude with your dentist. And once you get your extraction, you won't mind going to the dentist whenever you have to. You have a few more appointments yet, but all will be well."

"I'm working my way through my vanity, aren't I?"

"I do love your saying that life is a journey through vanity to humility. That has to be one of the most insightful sayings ever recorded. It speaks to the human condition like few sayings, capturing the essential journey of soul through life. This is the gist of Ecclesiastes' message, which we are going to explore in our sequel to your novel Healing with Padre Pio. *"*

"That's still on, then?"

"Yes. Early next spring we will be working diligently. By then you will have your two books finished—One Rule to Live By: Be Good, *and* Sundays with Sharon. *I'm looking forward to working together again. We have much to talk about."*

"I'd like to run something by you, if I may. I'm following the Jordan Peterson movement as he goes from city to city giving his talks on his book *12 Rules for Life: An Antidote to Chaos,* and I'm becoming very familiar with his message, and I have to tell you that I marvel at his genuine desire to help explain what the hell's going on out there; but I wonder why it's taken the world so long for someone like Jordan Peterson to come along. Can you tell me?"

"You ask a very deep question which is not easy to answer. It has to do with the evolution of society. What it took to conjoin the variables that wrought a Jordan Peterson would boggle your mind, but that's how the natural laws of evolution work. Nature has tried many times to conjure someone like Jordan Peterson to counter the forces of nihilism, and his appearance on the world stage is no accident, as you realize; but then, neither are you an accident. Your life is no less miraculous than Jordan Peterson's. Your message takes over where his leaves off. That's your contribution to literature, and the world. Keep writing, my friend. Your time is coming."

"Actually, I'm getting the itch again. It's only been a few weeks since I took my summer break to read the books that I have to read to complete *One Rule to Live By,* and already I'm starting to chomp at the bit. Maybe I should work on a spiritual musing or two?"

"By all means. Pay attention to the signs and symbols. I feel you will be getting something to write about within a few days. Just go with your nudges and hunches."

"My knee has improved. I'm about 90 percent there. I still have to be careful walking because my knee is still sore, but hopefully I'll be able to move around and get some more yard work done, and I also have some painting to do. I do want to do this for Penny. As to Jordan Peterson's message, I'm keeping a file on Peterson's message and the reaction to it, and I'm beginning to understand the nuances of political consciousness; but I can't help but wonder how the world can fall prey to such ideologies that can be responsible for so much suffering. But then, that's what motivated Jordan Peterson, isn't it? He had to know how people like Stalin and Hitler and Mao and other brutal dictators could do what they did, and still do; why are some people given to such evil? That was his need to know. That's why he wrote *Maps of Meaning,* which I'm in the process of reading. I'm only a quarter into it, and it's fascinating to see how he connects the dots; it gives me a great insight into his own individuation process, and I have to finish it before I get back to my book *One Rule to Live By: Be Good.*"

"Pay attention to this book. It will answer many questions for you. And it will give you exactly what you need to bring your own book to resolution. And you are correct to do what you are planning to do with all the articles you are keeping about Jordan Peterson. Do what you plan to do, study them and extract their essential message before you get back to One Rule to Live By, *because this will give you the gravitas you want for your book."*

"Will I ever get the language down?"

"Not as eloquently as you would like, but that is not your forte. You will be eloquent enough, but you will augment what you cannot articulate with your own philosophy. You will not be stumped when you are called upon, because you offer an entirely new perspective. And you will intrigue everyone no less than Jordan Peterson. You each have your own gifts."

"Until we talk again, then."

"Have a good day, my friend."

"Thanks, Padre…"

61. Extracting My Phobia

Wednesday, July 19, 2018

"Good morning, Padre. Today is the big day. Today I'm going to the dentist to have my phobia extracted. I've got a cracked molar that cannot be saved and I have to have it extracted, and with this extraction goes my phobia for dentists. I would like you there with me, Padre. I would like to have your healing, loving, compassionate energy with me, not only for myself but for everyone in the office. Your healing energy would do the place wonders. Will you, please?"

"It would be my honor. Yes, I will be there with you and for you and for everyone there; when asked, I cannot refuse. Thank you for asking."

"I'm hoping all will go well. After today's appointment, I have one more to go to next week; Thursday, I believe. For two more fillings. Then perhaps I can give my mouth a break and concentrate on my reading and thoughts on my writing."

"And so, it shall be. Yes, all will go well today, and next week. Just keep doing what you are doing. You are filling the well of your creative energies and eliminating all the anxiety and tension that impede the flow of the creative energies."

"I got my last Amazon book that I had ordered yesterday. *In Search of Taylor Caldwell,* by Jess Stearn. I started reading it the moment Penny brought it home, and I finished reading it this morning, and I'm terribly moved by it. It might just appear in my Jordan Peterson book."

"Yes, it will play a vital role in your point about reincarnation. This is why you were nudged to re-read your books on Taylor Caldwell."

"What do you think of my theory that I shared with Penny this morning, about the strata, or levels of consciousness co-existing in the world, how each strata of consciousness only sees and experiences life from that level of awareness, but all levels evolving simultaneously?"

A Sign of Things to Come

"You've pretty much got the ending for your Peterson book. This is how you are going to bring your book to its dialectical resolution. It will evolve more yet, but that will come as you do your summer reading. Keep notes as you read. They will come in handy."

"I don't know if you will answer this, but I suspect that Jordan Peterson may be the reincarnation of Carl Jung. Can you give me a hint?"

"This will be revealed to you in the fullness of time. He may be, he may not be; but he certainly could fit the profile of one who could be the incarnation of G. G. Jung."

"My poem 'What the Hell Is Going on Out There?' certainly got answered. Was my poem in any way contributory to the Jordan Peterson phenomenon?"

"He was called for a reason. Your poem put the question out there, and the Universe had to respond. That's how the creative unconscious works. Man has more power than he thinks."

"I really don't know what to say, Padre. I'm puzzled."

"You may be puzzled, but in your efforts to work out the puzzle you provide your reader with wonderful material to think about. You are blazing a new trail, my friend. Just keep doing what you are doing. This is your purpose."

"And so, I shall. Now I'm going to psyche myself up for my extraction."

"I will go and prepare the way for you."

"Thank you."

"You're welcome. All will be well. I promise…"

62. Extraction Postponed

Sunday, July 22, 2018

"Good morning, Padre. Well, my extraction got postponed because my blood pressure was too high; but Dr. Christina did two small fillings instead. So, I'm working on getting my blood pressure down for next week's appointment. I've cut out all coffee, alcohol, and salt, and I'm trying to do some cycling every day. And I'm glad to say it's working. I'm keeping a daily record of my blood pressure, and my little regimen seems to be working. But I'm going to start today by initiating a cucumber and celery smoothie, and lemon and garlic tea; these are supposed to be good for lowering blood pressure. But I have to go into Midland to purchase these products for my new regimen. Also, I've started drinking my Essiac tea again, morning and evening. Now, Padre, I have to tell you about our neighbor. She got bad news. She been diagnosed with cancer and is in a very dark place. Her husband shared this news with me the other day while I was on my front deck reading. He was walking his two little terriers and stopped to tell me. But while we were talking, Penny called from work and I quickly shared our neighbor's bad news with her, and Penny asked me if I had told him about Essiac tea, which has a history of curing cancer. I didn't, but I said I would, and I waited for my neighbor to walk around our street (Stocco Circle), and when I saw him approaching his driveway I called to him. He came down and I gave him my book on Essiac tea and the remaining package of dried Essiac herbs for his wife to make. And the next day, which was Saturday, I went into Midland to pick up my papers and sundries, and I thought to myself, wouldn't it be nice if my neighbors were walking their dogs when I come home so I can talk to her and give her my support. Well, Padre; I pulled into our yard, and as I got out of the car to put the fresh produce that I had picked up from Johnson's Market into the house, Tracy and Lenny were walking their two little terriers and I called out, "Tracy, come here," and as she walked over I put the produce on top of the freezer in our garage and then walked out to console Tracy. I held her in my arms and hugged her and said to her,

A Sign of Things to Come

"You can cry. It's alright..." And after a long consoling hug I saw that Penny had come out and she gave Tracy a hug also, holding her tight for a long while, and then we talked. Lenny left us to talk and walked up to his house with the dogs to discard his terrier's poop that he had picked on their walk, and then he came back down and he mostly listened while Tracy and I talked, with Penny adding a word or two here and there, but out of everything I said to Tracy, I told her to make friends with her cancer; and, I have to say, Padre, I think that was the best advice I could give her. And I told her that your energy was with me, and I gave her another healing hug when she left."

"Your compassion touched her heart so deeply that she will never forget you as long as she lives, and she will live longer than she now expects. Yes, you said all the right things, and she will get a great deal from the book you gave her. Marion Woodman's journal of her cancer experience will open your neighbor's eyes to a whole new world. She will become a different person because of her cancer experience, and she will have you to thank. You and Penny have shown Tracy and her husband that life is not all about the good life, and this is a realization that they were up against; now they've confronted it head on, and they thank you both for introducing them to a way of bringing some light into the darkness of their life. It moved me to tears to see how you and your loved one gave of yourselves to your neighbors. You touched them in a way that they will marvel over for years to come."

"I'm not going to ask, but I do hope that she comes through her dark night of the soul whole and intact."

"It's in God's hands, my friend. You did what you were called to do, and now God will do the rest. She's going to be doing a lot of re-adjustment, but this is what she needs to see the bigger picture. Have faith, my friend; all will be well."

"Padre, what a comfort to have you in my life. Thank you for listening."

"Thank you for inviting me into your life. We have come a long way together, and we will go a long way yet. Our journey is yet to be appreciated, but it will be. I promise."

"On that note, until we talk again."

"Ciao, my friend; and have a wonderful day..."

63. Shadow Pushback

"Good morning, Padre. If you will give me a few minutes, I'm going downstairs to put the coffee on; then we can have a little chat. I have something to tell you."

"Yes, I know. I can feel your disappointment…"

"I'm back, but I don't have a cup of coffee; I have a cup of herbal tea instead. Essiac, or what the natives call 'the tea of life.' I'm off coffee to get my blood pressure down so I can have my tooth extraction this Thursday. I've got my blood pressure down to an average of 155 over 90 for the five days that I've been monitoring it, and I think I should be good for Thursday. My dentist would like to see my maximum blood pressure at 150 over 109. She wanted me to see my doctor to get new medication, but I didn't want to go to the doctor and told her I would get it down myself. Anyway, Padre; what I want to talk to you about is our neighbor who was diagnosed with cancer. She's going for a biopsy today and Friday she's going for a cat scan and will know for sure how serious it is, but her husband told me yesterday that she made the Essiac tea that I had given her, after reading the book on Essiac that I had also given her to read, and she did brew the tea with the Essiac herbs that I also gave her, but then she went online and read up on Essiac and got scared off because of the possible side effects the tea could give her. Her husband told me yesterday that she might not take the tea now, and I couldn't believe my ears. But after some thought, I came to see that this was her shadow pushing back at the light, and I have to wonder at the incredible hold that her unconscious has on her. Padre, I kid you not, but I honestly do believe that life is a journey through vanity to humility. I fear she's got a tough road ahead of her."

"You are in a place of light, and light is terrifying to the shadow. It is not unexpected for the shadow to push back, but in time she will come to her senses. Be patient with her. Just let God do the

work. You have done yours. Be supportive, caring, and compassionate."

"May I ask you something very personal?"

"Yes."

"I fear I see her path. I know she is standing in her own way, and I can see the agony of her self-reconciliation. It will be a terrible pain, burning away her vanity with all the anguish of her cancer experience; but this is inevitable, because this is the natural way of evolution to wholeness and completeness. This is how life works. I want to ask if you could see with certainty a person's illness and the path they have to walk to burn the vanity that brought on the illness (and by vanity, I mean personal karma), and if this is so, I'd like to know how you were able to comfort them without being too truthful, if you know what I mean?"

"Yes, I could see with certainty; but it came gradually. You are growing in your second sight at a phenomenal pace, and your vision will become more and more precise, and I can tell you from my experience that it takes a lot of love and compassion to not be so revealing. You must remember that they are on their own path to God, and if you can help them in their self-reconciliation without shocking them, then do so. You can and will learn how to reveal the truth of their situation without shocking them. It takes love and compassion. Be gentle with her. She's not yet ready to embrace her illness. She's still in shock."

"I guess all I can do is let go and let God. I'll do my best to not frighten her with what I see, and just let my instincts guide me."

"I will be with you and guide you in your thoughts."

"Thank you. On to something else. My book *One Rule to Live By: Be Good*. I'm not through my reading yet, but I'm chomping at the bit to get back into it. I feel I've got a handle of what I want to say, and I can't wait to let my creative unconscious loose. But as I read what I've already written, I wonder at the readability of my story. It's too profound for the reader. What am I to do? I can't simplify it. This is the way it's coming out."

"This is your story. He told his, now tell yours. Don't apologize for it. It will find its readers just as his books found their readers."

"Okay. Good. Thank you for your insights. Until we talk again."

"I look forward to it. Have a nice day, my friend."

"You too, Padre…"

64. Today I'm (!) Old...

Tuesday, July 31, 2018

"Good morning, Padre. Today's my birthday, but I'm not going to say how old I am—as if that matters to you; but it does matter to me, in that dastardly vain way, which tells me that I've still got a way to go before I'm free of the vanity that's been my bane all of my life. But what am I to do? This is what I came into this world to work off, and believe me, have I been working it off—especially with my teeth issue. Boy, am I glad to have my dental appointments over with. Five appointments in five weeks, and I finally got my tooth extracted. This is such a good story that I'm going to work into one of my books. I don't know which one yet, but it may be *Sundays with Sharon*—unless my muse wants me to include it in *One Rule to Live By: Be Good.* Anyway, Padre; just thought I'd begin the first day of my birth year chatting with you."

"I'm glad that your extraction went well. Now you have no more phobia. This will ease the anxiety and set your mind free to be more creative. You're in a good place now, and you will have, as you foresaw, a very good creative winter. In fact, it will be one of the most creatively satisfying winters of your life, because you will be dreaded-phone call free now that you have sold your triplex. So, I look forward to chatting with you this coming winter. For now, what would you like to discuss. Anything. I'm free to expand your horizons."

"Wow. Seriously?"

"Yes."

"To tell you the truth, I'm really looking forward to working with you on the sequel to *Healing with Padre Pio*, which I hope to begin next spring. By then I hope to have my two books—*Sundays with Sharon* and *One Rule to Live By: Be Good* finished, and then I will be free to concentrate on our sequel. But let me ask you something. Am I getting more intuitive? I seem to think I'm growing in my—I hate to call it psychic, but that's what I think it is. Let's just say I'm getting more intuitive. Am I?"

"Either way is fine, and yes; you are. This is the nature of your progress. As you evolve in your own individuality, you grow in your intuitive ability. This is natural."

"Is that what happened to you? Is that how you became so intuitive that you could see into a person's soul and tell them what they needed to know, like I did with my neighbor who needed to know how to deal with her cancer?"

"Exactly. You told her what she needed to hear. You cut through a lot of time by telling her that, and she will be very thankful for your wisdom when she faces herself."

"Padre, I'm getting somewhat disheartened with the response to my book that I'm posting on my spiritual musings blog. I thought I'd pull in more viewers than I am. What's with that?"

"It will connect, I assure you. Just keep doing what you are doing."

"I've got a few books yet to finish reading for my book, but I'm beginning to get the insight that I need to feel confident in my perspective; but I'd like to ask you something, if I may. How can I own my knowledge the way Jordan Peterson does, or the way Carl Jung did?"

"You do. Your path is your way, your knowledge, your understanding. They own their path, their knowledge, their understanding; you simply need to frame your knowledge in a language that's more expansive, more inclusive, and that's why you were called to write One Rule to Live By: Be Good, *because writing this book will expand your intellectual paradigm that will allow you to express your path more inclusively, and less esoterically."*

"When will I experience that quantum leap that I'm looking forward to, that leap into the expansive horizons of my own individual way, if you know what I mean?"

"It's happening as we speak."

"I don't feel it. I'd like to know if it's possible for my literary personality to become my daily personality, if I will be free to express myself in daily conversation as I do when I am open to my creative unconscious to speak freely, because that's how I see Jordan Peterson?"

"Here's a tip. When speaking with people, don't gauge your conversation to suite what you think will be appropriate for them to

hear, just let your creative mind speak for itself. Don't measure your thoughts, let them speak freely. Do this a few times and you will see how Jordan Peterson speaks. This is his trick. He trusts himself implicitly."

"Can you be more specific?"

"Yes. Treat everyone as if you are speaking to me. Imagine every person you are speaking with as me, and let your mind speak freely. Try this and see what happens."

"I think you can be more specific yet."

"Do not censor your mind. Let your mind speak for itself. Do not tailor your comments for the benefit of another's feelings, or sentiments; just speak. Trust yourself implicitly. Your inner self knows what the other needs to hear, don't adjust your thoughts and feelings to what you think they need to hear or feel. Let God do that for you. That's Jordan Peterson's secret."

"Will this open the gates to my creative unconscious?"

"Yes."

"And is this the right way to go?"

"Why not? It's who you are, isn't it?"

"Yes. And it would be nice to be my whole self."

"And so, you shall be. You have asked, and now it will be so"

"I get the feeling that this is your birthday gift to me."

"It is. Your gift is to be your whole self in your daily personality. But you must take care to not let the river flow too swiftly, because you can be overwhelming. However, I will be with you to see that you flow to the fullness of appreciation. Happy birthday, my friend."

"Thank you, Padre.,."

65. Going up North

Sunday, August 5, 2018

"Good morning, Padre. Three words have popped into my mind: consolidate, consolidate, consolidate. The same word three times, not three separate words; the point being that I have to consolidate my energies, because I feel somewhat scattered. And I feel scattered because I have been too distracted with what's going on *out there*, in the world. I've been pulled out of my personal comfort zone, my own individuation process; that's why I have to consolidate my energies, to get back into the rhythm of my own journey through life. Right, or not?"

"Exactly so. You need to focus your attention to your writing. Your writing always pulls you back into the rhythm of your journey. Don't be distracted by the outside world. The outside world will always be there, fumbling its way towards its own end; but, as you like to say, life is an individual journey, so focus on that. You will get your focus back once you realign yourself with your destined purpose, which is to get your story into book form. Yours is an incredible story of self-revelation that needs to be told. Don't worry about the effect you will have, just do what you are called to do and let God take care of the rest."

"We're going up north this coming Friday to visit Penny's family, and I don't know if I'm going to drive through my hometown of Nipigon. I may just drive right on through. I have been severed from my ties to that town, and I feel free. I don't even want to see how our triplex is standing, if the new owner did anything with the supporting wall that needed mending. In all honesty, Padre; I'd like to just go right through and leave that part of my life behind me, unless I am called to write my novel *We May be Tiny, But We're Not Small.* I honestly don't know if I will ever get to write that story. Will I?"

"It's in your cards."

"Do I really want to get into why I don't want to stop off in Nipigon?"

A Sign of Things to Come

"You have earned your freedom. Exercise it."

"Here's a question. Reading my new work-in-progress *One Rule to Live By: Be Good* for editorial purposes, as well as my book *The Armchair Guru*, I can't help but see just how far outside the box I really am, and I'm left to wonder: who's going to read me?"

"More people than you think."

"I have to go to Marks Work Warehouse today to get some new pants, and perhaps a couple of polo shirts. I need them. I've worn my old jeans down and need new ones. I'm no longer interested in clothes like I used to be, but I should be more attentive. Anyway, I don't think I'm going to visit Sharon for tea this morning. I usually drop in Sunday mornings. She's the inspiration for my book *Sundays with Sharon*. I went picking blueberries with her several days ago. She picked me up. She had her friend Karen with her, who was up at her cottage. She's from Etobicoke. And our neighbour Jennifer came along too. I picked two baskets and got to talk with the owner of the blueberry farm. I think I may include our talk in my book *Sundays with Sharon*. It was coincidental to what I'm working on now, *One Rule to Live By: Be Good,* which is the twin soul book to *Sundays with Sharon*. Curious, what?"

"Very. And yes, you will include it in Sundays with Sharon. It will be an interesting chapter, more than you think."

"On the other hand, maybe I will visit Sharon this morning, because I won't see her for a few weeks. And after my visit, Penny and I can go shopping for some new clothes for me, which I need. God, I used to be so fussy with my clothes. What happened to me?"

"Your priorities shifted. As long as you are clean and presentable, what does it really matter? It's not the outer, it's the inner that matters. Take care of the inner and the outer will take care of itself. Do what you have to do, and let God take care of the rest."

"On that note, thank you Padre."

"You're welcome..."

66. The Humbling Begins

Wednesday, August 8, 2018

"Good morning, Padre. I have to share something. I hope I'm right in my perception, or I'm going to feel rather foolish. It has to do with our neighbor who was recently diagnosed with cancer. I'll get into this after Penny and I have our morning coffee. I just wanted to start this chat so I can focus my creative energies for the day. I hope you don't mind?"

"Not at all. We'll resume when Penny leaves for work..."

"Sorry, Padre; never got back to you yesterday. Maybe I didn't want to talk about the drama that I see unfolding in my neighbor's life, her cancer diagnosis and the humbling process that I see beginning to happen. I'd really like to include that observation in one of the current books that I'm writing. I don't know which one yet, but it sure would add gravitas to the book. And speaking of books, as I edit and tighten up *One Rule to Live By: Be Good,* I cannot help but feel that my perspective on life is so far beyond the reader that I just don't see my book connecting. Do you have anything you can tell me about this?"

"Every book has its readers, and so will your new book. It is deep for the average reader, but once they get into the flow of your logic they will deeply appreciate you. You must trust the process. By posting comments on Peterson's posts, you attract attention. One by one, you will get your book read, and read by millions."

"That's nice to hear. I don't know if I believe you, but all the same it sure makes me feel good and gives me the encouragement to complete it. Penny and I are leaving this morning for our little getaway up north to visit Penny's family in Thunder Bay, and I believe I'm going to drive straight through Nipigon, my hometown. I don't want to be reminded of my life there."

"That's where you changed your life for the different outcome that you sought. It gave you the experiences you needed to complete

what Nature could not finish. You are perfectly correct to not to want to be reminded, so just move on and let life unfold as it will."

"Penny and I were talking on our front deck yesterday, and I was reminded of the novels that I have written but are not yet published. I have five novels, Padre! And I'd like to have them published before I cross over. Will this happen?"

"Yes. No more needs to be said. Just do what you are called to do and let God take care of the rest. That's what you are meant to do."

"I sure hope our little trip up north will be as satisfying as I hope it will be, because this time we will be going up north on our terms. We've always gone up with the responsibility of our triplex on our mind, and often to take care of some triplex responsibility; but not this time, we are free to enjoy our little getaway, and I sure hope it turns out that way."

"It will, and even better than you hope."

"Here's a question I'd like to run by you, or a thought, if you will. I'm reading Nietzsche now and am getting a much better sense of what he's all about, and I cannot help but think that this brilliant man went off on a trajectory that took him to a philosophical perspective that did not see the whole picture, though he believed it was a large enough perspective to negate his nihilism, but, as Gurdjieff would say, he went from one prison into another; he trapped himself in his own non-being and died a brilliant, but mad fool."

"You're not far off the mark. Yes, he did take a trajectory that led him to a dead end, which he felt was the right end; but he failed to take into account the guiding principle of life that saves man from himself. He refused to be saved because of his hatred for Christianity. You will write a chapter for your book that will offer a way out of his dilemma. It will be one of your most important chapters. And when you write it, write it from the heart."

"Okay, Padre; I'm all packed. Just waiting for Penny to pack her luggage and we're on our way to our little getaway. We can chat when we get back."

"Have a safe journey, my friend. And don't worry."

"Ciao for now. Hope to get some material for my books."

"More than you think. Godspeed, my friend..."

67. Back from Our Getaway

Wednesday, August 22, 2018

"Good morning, Padre. Well, we made it up north safe and sound and we made it back safe and sound, and it proved to be a very interesting getaway, nothing like I expected; not that I expected anything in particular, but certainly not what we experienced. I don't know if I can go into the detail today, but I would like to run a thought by you on what happened on the evening of our arrival when I clashed with that young man with an attitude that needed correcting. We were all sitting in the gazebo by the pool at Penny's sister's house, where we were staying, and I don't really know how, but this young man (in his mid thirties) engaged himself in a conversation that I was having with his fiancé, the mother of Penny's sister's grandchild, the one I recognized as a star child, which is what his mother and I were talking about when her fiancé cut in with strong opinion that I had to respond to because his spiritual obtuseness annoyed me, but it didn't make for a pleasant evening because it upset Penny so much she wanted to pack our bags and leave the next day; so, what happened? Did my energy clash with that wall of spiritual obtuseness that rankled me? What happened, Padre?"

"Your light was much too bright for his eyes, and the eyes of most everyone there. The only one who saw your light was the star child, and Penny Lynn. That young man needed a reality check, as you said; and he got one. That was a long time coming for him, because he's been getting away with his attitude for much too long. He needed to hear what you said to him, and don't worry about the consequences. It did the rest of them good too."

"That whole thing inspired a thought for a spiritual musing, or a chapter in *One Rule to Live By*, a chapter called "The Great Choreographer of Life." I don't know whether to write it up as a spiritual musing or as a chapter."

"Write it up as a spiritual musing first and see what happens."

A Sign of Things to Come

"I have to share something else with you. I don't believe it was a coincidence because I think the choreographer of life arranged it, but I discovered a new poet on this trip. Penny and her younger sister went to the market to pick up a few vegetables for the family dinner that she was making and they came upon a booth with a young poet/musician/photographer selling his books and 2019 Calendar with his nature photos. Penny's sister bought the calendar, which she gifted me, and Penny bought his book of poetry, which she gifted me; and I loved them both, but the book of poetry engaged me from the first three lines— "Take a chance, /dig deeper, /take more risks." These lines begin his poem "Advice." Well, Padre; I read most of the book and I see this young man is desperately struggling to give birth to his inner self, and my heart goes out to him. I just sent him a Facebook friend request this morning, and I hope to engage him in a conversation; but I feel that this young man is going to make it into my book *One Rule to Live By.* Am I right in this feeling?"

"Very much so. That's why it was meant for you to discover him. This is what your book needs to bring it to resolution, a real person who is looking for direction and purpose, and your other books are what he needs to make sense of his lifelong journey. It was meant to be, and you can thank the divine choreographer of life for this."

"On our way home Monday morning, we stopped off in Dorion to visit Penny's sister's mother-in-law, who just turned ninety, to give her my book *The Pearl of Great Price.* She's read a number of my books and loves my writing. It nourishes her soul's longing, and we had a very satisfying visit. "You gave me a nice shot in the arm," she said to me, with a big smile; and Penny and I left happy for stopping by. Strangely enough, I had planned to give her two of my other books, my book of poetry, *Not My Circus, Not My Monkeys,* and *The Merciful Law of Divine Synchronicity,* but for some reason I was nudged to give these away to other people, which left me with *The Pearl of Great Price* to give to Marg; so, was that choreographed too?"

"It most certainly was. That was the book for her at this time in her long life. She will find this book the most satisfying of all of your other books that she has read, and she will be very grateful that

you stopped by to visit her and her daughter. Her daughter loves your writing also, and she is learning a great deal from your writing."

"I also visited my friend Tarmo when we were in Thunder Bay. We went out three times and had some wonderful talks. I gave him my books *My Writing Life,* which is the sequel to *The Lion that Swallowed Hemingway*, which I gave him three years ago when we last visited, and also a copy of *The Merciful Law of Divine Synchronicity*, and he told me something that I thought was rather interesting. He told me that the first time he read *The Lion that Swallowed Hemingway,* he didn't really care for it that much; but he read it again, and he got a whole new perspective, saying that it must have spoken to him because he had changed. Well, he is going through a transformative experience with his wife who went through cancer treatment and is still not out of the woods yet, so my book affected him differently on the second reading. Does one have to have a confrontation with the mortality of life before they appreciate what I write, or what?"

"The short answer is yes. People are much too caught up in their life to stare into the face of their own mortality. Although your friend is a realist, your writing pulls no punches, and as he went through his transformation because of his wife's illness, he got a different read on your book, and he's much more appreciative of your writing now."

"Okay, Padre; that's all for now. I'm thinking of starting my spiritual musing, so I want to save my creative energy for that. Thanks for the chat. Anything you want to tell me?"

"Focus. Write. This is your imperative. Until we talk again."

"*Ciao* for now, then—Oh! I just thought of something. I did a lot of reading when I was on our getaway, and I got into Nietzsche, and I think I may have figured out what I have to write about to offer a way out of his dilemma. But I want to ask you something about him. He made the eternal return the theme of his book *Thus Spoke Zarathustra*, making *amor fati* (love of fate) central to his philosophy; but, as you told me, I came back to live my same life over again, so this concept of the eternal return is real to me (I wrote about this in *The Summoning of Noman*). I did relive my life over again, and I did so to achieve a different outcome. Is this going to be the theme of my chapter on Nietzsche in my *One Rule to Live By* book?"

A Sign of Things to Come

"Exactly. You will offer hope for the reader. This is going to be coupled with your reading of the young poet you were introduced to, and the theme of your chapter will be the birthing of the self. No more need be said."

"Thank you…"

68. A Consolidating Experience

"Good morning, Padre. I took a sleeping pill last night, so I'm a little groggy this morning; but I do want to run something by you about our little trip up north which was fraught with an energy that Penny is still processing. I suspect I know what the underlying current between her and her sister was all about, but I'm not at liberty to say. However, I know that you know and I have to ask you, was all the psychic tension the result of resolving shadow energy?"

"Yes, you could put it like that without offending anyone. It had to be done. This was what caused all the fuss, and now that it's over you and Penny's sisters can begin with a clean slate, they to resolve their own issues and you and Penny to continue in your own life on your own terms. You and Penny have earned your retirement, and you will enjoy your life in your little corner of joyful plenitude with the grace that will be an inspiration for some and cause for resentment for others. Your acknowledgement of Penny's younger sister's new job was a gesture that spoke of your character, and it went a long way to expressing who and what you really are, and it was cause for joy for some and resentment for others. You will be exploring this emotion of resentment in One Rule to Live By: Be Good. *You are only a few chapters from completing the book, and you have gotten a good start with your latest spiritual musing."*

"Okay, now I come to the consolidating experience. That word 'consolidating' popped into my mind when I explained what my trip up north was like, and although the words that come to me to explain something are more often than not the right words for the context, I had to look it up for confirmation; and the word 'consolidate' means: *to join together into one whole: unite; to make firm or secure: strengthen; to form into a compact mass.* This is the word that my creative unconscious chose to describe my experience up north, and now I'm going to explain why and how this happened, if you would like to hear?"

A Sign of Things to Come

"I know what happened, but for the sake of A Sign of Things to Come, *please tell me; and I will add to what you have discerned, because there was much more going on than even you realized."*

"It started with my not wanting to stop off in Nipigon to see our old town and the triplex that we sold. I did not want to drive through that town, which I have described as my little corner of hell that I was thrown into to find my lost soul. Let's start with that. Am I right in this, or am I being dramatically creative?"

"Not at all. Everyone has to be somewhere, and your poem Noman *gave you the insight you needed to see where you had to be to find your lost soul. So, yes; you had good reason to not want to drive through your old town. You wanted to stay disconnected from the energy of that town since you had no more ties to it after you sold your triplex."*

"But wouldn't you know it. As we were driving down the Trans Canada Highway through my old hometown, guess who appeared at the end of their driveway as we drove by? Our friends Nancy and Sam. Was that divine timing, or what? Nancy was the person who introduced me to that New Age spiritual teaching that Penny and I walked away from four years ago, a teaching that I lived for more than thirty years but which I finally came to accept as a fraudulent teaching built upon a fabricated lie by a very clever man, and even though Nancy and her husband Sam also left this teaching shortly after Penny and I did, I did not want to stop and say hello to them; but I didn't feel right, because Nancy had called me just the month before, and I felt guilty for not stopping to say hello when I saw them in their driveway. So, we drove on, but they pulled out of their driveway on their way to their cottage, and as they followed us on the way out of town, I relented and asked Penny to pull over on the road to their cottage; but then the strangest thing happened. Penny pulled over and I got out, and as Nancy pulled onto the road to their cottage I waved and Penny waved and I got out and waved again and Penny even honked the horn, and as they drove by they stopped the car for a second or two and waved to us and then continued driving, not recognizing us at all; and this gave me the sign I needed that the great choreographer of life did not want us to reconnect with those energies from the past. Right, or not?

"Yes. You did the right thing to stop, but it wasn't meant for you to reconnect with those energies from the past; it was meant for you to break clean, which is what set the whole tone for your stay in Thunder Bay, because you were now free to be yourself without the energy from your past haunting you. You made a choice to severe from that energy, and you began to come out in full force for the person that you had worked so hard to become; that's why you were so forceful in your conversation that evening at Penny's sister's home with her guests. You had no patience for nonsense, and you played your hand without any apologies. You had come unto your own, working with your own unfettered energies; and you shocked everyone. But that young man needed a wake-up call, and you gave it to him. This was the beginning of your consolidating experience that continued until you left for home."

"But wasn't it strange that Nancy and Sam did not recognize us?"

"It was meant to be. The divine choreographer took care of that because you asked divine spirit to do what was best for you, and God chose for you to sever your ties with them and the town where you had to look for your lost soul. Now you are free of that energy."

"As well as with Penny's sister. I feel that I consolidated my energies with her, despite how traumatic it turned out to be. She had no idea what was going on, because it was all on the subconscious level; but I did. And also with my friend Tarmo, who never really could get a handle on what I am; but because of his wife's cancer, he changed enough to see my writing in a whole new light, which was why he said that his re-reading of *The Lion that Swallowed Hemmingway* spoke to him the second time around, and I gave him my sequel, *My Writing Life*, and he read twelve chapters before Penny and I left for home, and he saw and read me in a whole new light now. That was very consolidating for me."

"Yes, it certainly was. And he's very grateful for your friendship. And so is his wife."

"And I got introduced to a young poet's work through a remarkable coincidence which I've already written about in a spiritual musing called "When the Student is Ready..." I'm going to be including this musing on my new chapter of my Peterson book, *One Rule to Live By: Be Good*. I may do a little more work on it today, or I may not. I picked up three boxes of Roma tomatoes at the Superstore yesterday, and Penny and I are going to can them today."

"Do your canning and enjoy your day."

"Is there anything you would like to share with me about our trip up north?"

"Only that you both needed that trip to come to terms with your own little corner of joyful plenitude. You now realize how fortunate you are, and this is cause for resentment for those who are not big enough to acknowledge your accomplishments. Just remember that. Even with the people down here, your neighbors and friends. Be attentive. But don't let resentment get to you. Give love back and let the world work out its own problems. This is life. As you have been writing about for years, just be a good person and let God take care of the rest. Now get on with your day, and if you work on your book or not doesn't matter. You will after you get your tomatoes canned and other chores done. You are in God's hands, my friend."

"Thank you, Padre.

"You're welcome..."

69. Can We Talk, Please?

Monday, August 27, 2018

"I have a need to talk with you, Padre; but, honestly, I don't know what to say. I feel like there's something that I have to run by you, but I can't seem to work out what it is. I put coffee on this morning, and as I waited for my first cup of coffee I tried to get into Peterson's book *12 Rules for Life: An Antidote for Chaos*, which I feel I should read again to better understand it for my own book *One Rule to Live By: Be Good,* but I couldn't get past the first page; I just did not have it in me, with the thought that I shouldn't bother reading anymore and just write my book. It's as though I've done enough reading and should just write. What is that about?"

"It's exactly how it feels. You are tired of reading about other people's experiences and you feel your experiences are as worthy if not more to write about. That's why you have no desire to read anything. Not today, anyway. Tomorrow you may feel different. But that should not negate your feeling of being worthy enough to write your own experiences. Just go with the feeling and see where it takes you."

"I guess I'm still processing our experience up north. Penny told me last night while we were sitting on the deck that the best time she had on her time off work was the three hours she spent on the deck the other night watching the moon. She said she felt like all the nonsense that she experienced up north washed out of her and she felt so good that she could hardly believe it. I don't want to discuss her relationship with her sister, but whatever it was it made her stay in Thunder Bay anxious and difficult, so much so that she was willing to pack our bags and leave the day after we arrived. I need not say anymore. My stay however proved very satisfying, because I consolidated my life up north; and by that, I mean that things fell into place for me on that trip, and I feel that I resolved my feelings about my life in my hometown of Nipigon and can now move on with my life down here. I really am a Georgian Bay boy now, Padre; and I feel good about having consolidated my feelings about my life up north. In fact, this feeling of consolidation has given me an inner confidence about myself that is translating into writing confidence. Is this why I feel that I need not read and just write? Not that I don't want to read, it's just that I feel I don't need to read; I can just write my own books in the confidence of my new sense of personal consolidation. Does that make sense to you?"

"Very much so. I did not get this feeling until I was blessed with the holy wounds of Jesus, which gave me the confidence to know that I was doing what I prayed for, to be a servant of our Lord and Savior. Once I embraced my destiny, I was on my way to personal consolidation. You had to experience much to become who you are, and it all came together for you when you and your love went up north to visit her family. This trip put it all together for you, and you came home to Georgian Bay fully resolved in your new life. Embrace it. Live it. Write and write and write to your heart's content, because you are free of all the obstacles that hindered you. This is the beginning of a new chapter in your writing life, and it will be very fulfilling."

"Yesterday Penny and I canned some tomatoes. On Saturday I picked up three boxes of Roma tomatoes for four dollars a box at the Superstore in Midland (at four dollars a box, it was a gift that I could not refuse), but our pressure canner leaked air and I tried to seal the gasket with silicone, which didn't work because when I shut the lid we couldn't get it off and I broke the handles trying to open it; so I had to drive into Midland to buy a pot to water-bath the jars, and we did twenty-one jars and the rest we're going to do today. I had to buy three more boxes of jars, but despite all the frustration it's going to be worth it. Besides, it got Penny's mind off her trip up north which she's still trying to process. Anyway, today I'm going to prepare the rest of the tomatoes for canning, and to relax I'm going to finish reading my weekend papers. I'm not quite ready yet to get into my book *One Rule to Live By*, but I will in a day or so."

"You were right when you told Penny that your little inconveniences yesterday with your canning were the cumulative result of your experience up north. It was a way of working out the energies of your trip, and all will be well today because all of your frustrations dealing with your canning issues worked out the energy

that needed to be worked out. Today things will go much more smoothly because you are in a new rhythm."

"About my dreams last night. Am I working through some old feelings in my hometown of Nipigon? What's with the sexual experience with that older woman I had a mad crush on? Did I have to work it out on the inner to resolve my feelings?"

"Yes. It had to be worked out. Now you can both move on. She too had a crush on you, but now it is worked out and you can both move on with your life."

"Is this how it works, what we can't work out in the outer we can work out in our dreams?"

"Yes, for those who are on the path. Those who are not yet on the path will have to carry their karma from one lifetime to the next until they are blessed to be initiated into their path. It is a gift for one to be initiated into the way. The path takes your life and brings it to resolution, both in the outer and the inner. But this is a deep mystery for another time."

"Here's a feeling that I've come home with from our little getaway: I'm no longer troubled by the troubles of the world. I feel that the world is what it is, and it will always be what it is according to its own karmic logic, and there's nothing I can do about it but watch how the world unfolds and do my best to make my little corner of the world better. I feel free of any obligation to make the world a better place, just my own little corner of the world."

"That's the way it's meant to be. This is what it means to live your own path. You will be sharing this perspective in your new book. It will make sense in the context of your theme of only one rule to live by, which is to be good. I love this book. I can see the finished book, and it will surprise you how it is going to be received. I promise.

"For the good, I hope."

"How else?"

"I don't think I have that much more to write. Maybe three or four more chapters and it will be finished. I have to work myself back into the zone, which I will do by reading everything I've written so far, then I will get back into the Peterson interviews and lectures so I can saturate myself with his logic so I can bring my book to resolution. Is that how it's going to be?"

A Sign of Things to Come

"Yes. Your postings will generate interest. Give it three or four more postings on your blog and then someone will share your post and this will get the ball rolling."

"That's what I'm waiting for. Until then, I'll just keep doing what I'm doing; so, until we talk again, thank you Padre for listening."

"You're welcome…"

70. Terrifying Dream Last Night

Wednesday, August 29, 2018

"Good morning, Padre. I had another one of those dreams last night, a dream in which I am lost, usually in a strange city, and I can't find my way home. In last night's dream I lost my luggage and my way and I couldn't get any direction from anybody and I had no phone numbers to call and it was frightening to be lost in a strange city, and I woke up very disturbed. I've come to see these dreams as a starting over, as though my unconscious is telling me I have outgrown my place (my state of consciousness) and am looking for a new place to dwell, but not knowing what this place is, I am frightened. I'm in a place between states, if I can express it this way; and I attribute this to our visit up north where I came to terms with my life up there, my hometown with which I no longer have any ties since we sold our triplex, and I feel great relief for severing all of my ties to that town; but in my dream I'm in a strange city, and I think severing my ties with my hometown has left me in a place where I need a new city to dwell in, if I can express it this way. In short, Padre, I'm in desperate need of a new state of consciousness that will accommodate the changes that I experienced on our trip up north which consolidated my feelings about my life up there. Any insight you have to offer will be greatly appreciated."

"Your dream last night was one of orientation. You are about to enter into a new phase of spiritual growth, all due to the consolidating experience you had up north. You're about to enter into a new state of consciousness that will astound you. You have begun to feel it already. This is the feeling you have of not really caring about life as you see it around you. It's not that you don't care, you simply see it for what it is and this separates you from life. This is a new state of non-attachment, a state of being apart from life in a way that is difficult for you to describe; but you cannot relate to life like you used to. You were always different from others, but now you are so far apart in your understanding of life that you feel almost alien. You are

not alien. You are just more evolved. You have transcended yourself again, this time to a place where you can see the oppressive burden of human consciousness. This is your dream in a nutshell. You were lost in the oppressive consciousness of life, and it frightened you. Now that you have seen it, you are about to enter a new phase of self-realization consciousness."

"Thank you. Anyway, Penny and I canned 60 jars of tomatoes Monday and Tuesday, and last night we made 12 jars of peach jam, and my body aches all over. I want to get back into my writing zone, but I don't think I'm ready yet. I'm just going to phase into it slowly, reading my book to where I left off. I have to get back into the feel of my story. I do have to tell you that you may be right about me, feeling apart as I do now, because even when I listen to the Jordan Peterson interviews I feel like it's all old hat, and I want to move on; but I can't. I have to enter into that state of consciousness to finish my book. Or do I?"

"You can't even if you tried. You have come back from up north consolidated, which makes you the individual that you have wanted to be your whole life, free to be yourself; that's what happened when you got into that argument with Clyde the evening that you and Penny arrived in Thunder Bay. You were yourself, uninhibited by the double brandies that you had, and you let it all out. Metaphorically speaking, you let the genie out of the bottle and you cannot put it back again. This is why you feel so apart from life now. But you will get used to this new perspective, and it will be the place from where your writing will come. So, you can't really get back into that same zone, as it were; you will be finishing your book from this new state of self-realized consciousness, and it will have all the gravitas of your new state of consciousness to give it the moral weight it needs for the message of being a good person."

"Pardon me saying this, but I honestly feel like the world around me is stuck in a state of stupefying idiocy, and if it weren't so tragic it would be hilarious."

"The circus goes on and the monkeys never stop playing. This is the tragedy of man's blind selfishness that reduces life to wants, needs, desires, and cruelty. But the divine spark in man needs to be realized, and it struggles to see the light; this is the saving grace of the human race. Without the divine spark man would have destroyed

197

himself long ago. The divine spark in man is the moral imperative that corrects man's behavior. This is the underlying theme of your book One Rule to Live By: Be Good. *You will have it finished before the New Year and you will have it published in the spring. It will be a very satisfying experience, all the way around; and it will be the start of a whole new period in your writing career."*

"Okay, thank you Padre. I have to wake Penny up now. Until we talk again."

"Have a nice day, my friend.'

"I hope to…"

71. Lost Again in a Strange City

Thursday, September 6, 2018

"Good morning, Padre. I woke up lost again. I was in a strange city in my dream last night and I woke up not knowing where I was, and I didn't have my watch; some keen pickpocket had taken it from my wrist without me knowing, or so I think. And it was getting to be night as I looked for my way back, to where I didn't know; all I knew was that I was lost again, and I'm beginning to get tired of this theme. What the hell is going on, Padre?"

"What did you listen to this morning on the radio? Wasn't it one of your favorite programs? Ideas, with Paul Kennedy? Didn't he interview the author of the new book 21 Lessons for the 21st Century? *Didn't that book give you the impression that the author was lost in the world of his own mind, a world that he believes to be more real than the world he's analyzing? Don't you think he's the one who's lost, and not you?"*

"As a matter of fact, I do. The author, Yuval Noah Harari (I have his previous book *Homo Deus, A Brief History of Tomorrow*, which I never got to finish reading because it annoyed me) came across with the most pessimistic perspective on life that I've heard in a long time; so, thank God that I had just finished reading a great chunk of Carl Jung's *Memoirs, Dreams, Reflections*, because reading Jung is like snuggling up in a warm, cozy blanket—that's how comfortable and secure he makes me feel with his understanding of life and the human condition. So, are you saying that I'm somehow tapping into the consciousness of today's lost souls, like Yuval Noah Harari who has zero insight into the divine and immortal nature of the human soul and can see no meaning to life other than to ward off those corporate forces that seek to enslave us?"

"Yes. This is to motivate you to write your own books to counter these negative impressions of life that writers like Harari are promulgating. Life is not all about desire and wants and needs and getting the most out of it before one's body dies; life is about growth

and understanding, and it is your calling to let the world know that the purpose of life is to realize one's divine nature. This is why you keep getting lost in your dreams. Your unconscious is letting you know that the world has lost its way and you have to help the world find its way. And your lost watch. That's a symbol to let you know that time is relative to the individual. Losing your watch is symptomatic of the world's lost time, the time the world spends on the wrong path, like Harari's thinking about the human condition. It's a very pessimistic point of view."

"Well, he is a Jew after all—"

"Yes, he is; and pessimism is a national trait. But as humorous as that may be, what he's writing will affect a lot of people. So, what can we do about it?"

"You're asking me?"

"Yes."

"Finish my book *One Rule to Live By: Be Good*. This book offers a completely opposite perspective. That life is divine in essence, and our purpose in life is to become what we are meant to be—spiritually self-realized souls. That's all I can do."

"That's enough. Write your book and get it finished. You are almost ready to jump back into the zone. A few more days and you will be back into it full force."

"Can I ask you something about Carl Jung?"

"Yes."

"Why does he make me feel so good when I read him?"

"Carl Jung is an amazing soul. He broke the code of the secret way and he gave it to the world in his psychology of individuation. You broke the code of the secret way and you identify with everything he says, or everything that you understand about what he says, because Carl Jung explored regions of the soul that will take you years yet to understand; but you also discovered regions of the soul that he is learning from also. That's the nature of your relationship with him. You meet him on the inner planes quite often, though you do not know it."

"Okay, thank you Padre. I'm going to get my first cup of coffee now, and then I'm going to read and edit and ponder on my book *One Rule to Live By*. Until we talk again."

"Ciao, my friend..."

72. From Order to Chaos

Tuesday, September 18, 2018

"Padre, please bring Penny back home to me safe and whole. That was my plea to you from the moment I collected my senses enough to reason somewhat clearly after Penny was hospitalized with bleed on the brain, an aneurism that she had to have operated on at St. Michael's Hospital in Toronto this past Sunday, the day after the blood vessel in her brain burst and she cried out with so much pain that it scared our neighbors; but thank God they were home to help her, because I was in Midland getting my papers and groceries. The operation has been done and there appears to be no effects to her cognition or motor skills and I just don't know how to thank you for answering my plea for help. I pleaded with you, 'Please Padre, bring Penny back home to me safe and whole.' She's not home yet and won' t be for a while because she's still in ICU at St. Michael's, but so far it looks very hopeful, and I just want to thank you and ask you formally now to please be with her all the way through her crisis. I need her, Padre. I need my Penny Lynn because I have not yet begun to love her the way she deserves to be loved. Please, please bring her back home to me safe and whole."

"My heart goes out to you, my good friend, and I promise that your loved one will come home to you safe and whole. You have to experience what you have to experience so you can love each other whole and complete. This is the lesson of your life together. Please do not worry about her life. She will come home to you safe and whole. It is in her soul contract."

"THANK YOU!"

"You're welcome. You will both have a complete change of attitude with each other and with life. This experience will have opened your heart to such a level of compassion and understanding that you will be shining examples of being what people should be, good and loving and kind and considerate and caring, just as Jeshua

said in his message to Glenda in her book The Keys of Jeshua. This book will be your bible for the rest of your life."

"I've already made the 'community prayer' MY prayer. It spoke to what I'm going to aspire to, which I hope will endow me with the virtues that you just outlined."

"You will, and much more. Your writing will also take on much more depth with your newfound awareness. As difficult as this experience has been and will be for the next few days until Penny is fully cognizant and able to remove your fear you will survive, and your love for Penny will multiply by the day. It warms my heart to see your love for each other."

"The love you see growing when Penny comes home safe and whole?"

"Yes, and even now your love for her has grown beyond your expectations. And your compassion for others has grown also, as you illustrated with your appreciation for your neighbor who fed your fish and took care of other things in your house while you were at St. Michael's Hospital in Toronto. Please do not worry, my friend. I promise all will turn out well and the world will unfold for you and your loved one and you both will fulfill your destiny."

"I'd like to give details of what happened, but not now. You know what happened, and that is all that matters. Thank you, Padre. And please be there for Tracy and Lenny as you are here for Penny Lynn and me. They are good people, and it would be so nice to see them find some measure of peace and resolution with Tracy's medical situation. I won't say any more about this now because this is not the place for this. This is a personal plea to you to bring my Penny Lynn back home to me safe and whole. Thank you for being there for me, Padre. I needed you and pleaded with you and Penny appears to be safe and whole, but as her tending nurse said yesterday, 'She's not out of the woods yet.' Please be with her every step of the way as she steps out of the woods of her medical situation."

"I am with her as we speak and will be with her for the rest of her life, and yours. We have much to do yet, so please continue to grow in love and understanding, and write your books. This is your destiny. Now read your book and have your coffee and get on with your day."

"Again, thank you Padre."

A Sign of Things to Come

"You're welcome. I will let Penny know that I am with her.
"She would love that. Thank you…"

73. Please Bring Her Back to Me Safe and Whole

Wednesday, September 19, 2018

"Good morning, Padre. My neighbors have graciously offered to drive me to Oakville where I'm going to be staying with my sister while Penny is in the ICU at St. Michael's Hospital in Toronto. She's not out of the woods yet and I have to be there for her. I broke down yesterday when my sister called. She reached out to me and offered to be there for me in my time of need. Padre, I broke down. *"I need you, Mary,"* I cried, sobbing like—I don't know what; a man whose life has been shattered, or broken, or so gravely disrupted that I didn't know where to turn? But I do have amazing neighbors, Tracy and Lenny, who drove me to St. Michael's to be there when Penny came out of her operation, and they picked me up again the next day; and this morning they're going to drive me to my sister Mary's in Oakville, where I will be staying to be close to Penny in her time of need. I have to be there, Padre. And I have asked you to be there for her too. And I keep pleading with you to bring her back to me safe and whole, and I feel almost assured that she will be; but I have to rid myself of the doubt that remains. Help me, please."

"Your doubt is natural in these circumstances. Do not make more of it than what it is. It is out of your deep love for Penny that your doubt arises, and this is not a bad thing. It confirms your love for her. She will come out of the woods and come home safe and whole and you will love each other unconditionally, which is the object of this painful experience. And the effect of this experience has already begun to affect your friends and neighbors and family in a way that only a miracle can; so please be happy for all the healing."

"I'm beginning to see that, and I am tickled pink; but I can't wait to have Penny home so I can take care of her."

"She will be home and you will take care of her. You have your golden years to live."

"I'm so thankful that I can do Lenny's garage. He's hanging drywall and I offered to tape it, and this makes me feel good because he and Tracy have been so good to me. They didn't even hesitate to take me to St. Michael's Hospital. I would never have attempted to drive to Toronto. But Lenny is like Captain Kirk in command of The Star Ship Enterprise; that's how much confidence I have in his driving through Toronto. And, as I said, they are going to pick me up at ten o'clock this morning to drive me to my sister's in Oakville; and from there I can take the Go Transit to St. Michael's Hospital every day so I can be with Penny. And my neighbor Colin is going to feed our goldfish Goober. I'm leaving our house key with Colin. He and his wife Jennifer probably saved Penny's life by calling 911; but I can talk about this another time. So, Padre; thank you for being there with me, and did you hear my request?"

"Yes, I will guide you in your path of unconditional love. It will be my greatest joy. I've been waiting for this day, and now it's here. My friend, go to your loved one and give her a kiss and tell her that we are with her and will always be with her. Ciao for now, my friend.

74. Where do I Start?

"I have so much to say. Where do I start, Padre?"

"What does your heart say?"

"My heart says thank you for Penny's healing. I prayed to you, asking you to bring her back home to me safe and whole, and she is home now safe and whole. She's still weak from her operation and will need time to heal, and I have to thank you for answering my prayers, and Jesus, and God."

"Welcome back, my son. It's been a long journey back to your roots, and even though you have found the answers you sought you no longer need to worry about which path to take because you have experienced the only path there is, the path of love. Your love for Penny initiated you into the mystery of love, and that was the reason that your loved one chose to have her experience. It was in her Soul contract."

"To send me to the dark side of the moon?"

"Yes. But you came back whole and intact. You experienced more life in one month than you have in the past ten years. That was the nature of your experience. And now you can resolve all your differences and love without prejudice."

"I'm afraid, Padre. I fear I may not have it to do what I feel I have yet to do. I want to honor my love for Penny by making her life as comfortable as I can, fulfilling all of my life obligations with her which I have avoided all these years; can I honor my promise to her? I fear my health may not hold up. I fear many things."

"Of course, you fear. You have just come back from the dark side of the moon, and the memories of the dark side are still vivid. Give yourself some time to compose yourself. You will get it all together within a month or two. I promise."

"I was very vulnerable during Penny's hospital experience, and I'm afraid everyone saw just how vulnerable I was. I blubbered and broke down to my family, and I just don't know what to make of my vulnerability. Does it make me look weak?"

A Sign of Things to Come

"Your vulnerability was necessary for your family and friends. They saw that you are as human as the rest of the world, and this was as good for them as it was for you. This is how you grow in wisdom and understanding. I'm proud of you, my son."

"My son?"

"Yes, my spiritual son. You sought me out, and I was there for you. You needed my help, and I was there for you. You prayed to Jesus, and he was there for you. You prayed to God, and God was there for you. A spiritual son or daughter is one who has surrendered to the Divine, and it pleases me to know that you were called to the final surrender. This will be a closing chapter in your new book, by the way. You will get back into it in a week or so, and you will bring it to closure before the New Year."

"I fear to ask, what will come of this book?"

"Let the book find its own destiny. I assure you, it has one much greater than you can imagine. It will go a long way to explaining the final mystery."

"Padre, I feel like crying."

"Yes, I know. Crying is good for the soul. It washes away the emotions that hold you back from what you need to grow in wisdom and understanding. Get some rest. Go by the fire and read your book Love without End, Jesus Speaks. *It will comfort you."*

"I will. Thank you."

"Everything will be fine. I promise…"

75. Not Quite There Yet...

"Good morning, Padre. I'm not quite there yet, but hopefully soon. And by 'there' I mean my normal creative state which got interrupted by my journey to the dark side of the moon with Penny's brain aneurism, neurosurgery, and recovery—a blessed miracle, for which we are eternally grateful. Thank you again for being there for us. I don't think I have even begun to process this one in a million experience—"

"The odds are exceedingly much more than one in a million, such was the nature of Penny Lynn's experience. Good morning, my friend. Yes, it has been a very strange journey, going to the dark side of the moon and back. Just as you said to your friend Lenny yesterday, everything is the same but different now, and it is from this state of difference that your writing will come from. That is why your psychic friend Nanette was told by her inner guide for you to plant a new acorn seed. This will be your new life-tree, an oak tree of literature written from this same but different state of consciousness; and, believe me when I tell you this, you will enjoy this creative period of your life much more than you have ever enjoyed writing."

"What? Writing short stories, novels, poetry?"

"Yes. Primarily short stories and novels. This will be your new life-tree."

"Within the context of my life obligations, which I promised Penny to fulfill; only then will I have the peace of mind to write guilt free."

"Yes. You will see to all of your life obligations with Penny Lynn, and this will expand your relationship immeasurably. And yes, I can hear the summoning voice of this book calling it to closure, with a new title (A Sign of Things to Come); but we will continue our dialogues in another volume. So, please do not exhaust yourself trying to capture Penny's miracle in your writing so soon. It will come when it comes, and not before. Let your heart work its way to the meaning

of this miraculous experience, and when the time is right it will find its way into the story that needs to be written."

"I'm tempted to bring *One Rule to Live By: Be Good* to closure with a chapter called 'The Dark Side of the Moon.' Will that work?"

"Yes, but let your muse work it out for you. You have to get back into the rhythm of this book before you write the closing chapter. Only then will it bear fruit."

"Read my manuscript completely before getting back into it?"

"Yes. Carefully, with editorial changes as needed. Don't worry. This book has its own destiny which will call it the moment it is finished. This, I guarantee."

"I have no doubt, Padre. You've come through on everything that you have said to me, so why not this?"

"Alright, my friend; why not end this volume here, then?"

"And so, we shall. Thank you for being there for me, Padre. I mean this from the depths of my wounded heart and soul. Whether you are a figment of my imagination, my Philemon, an archetypal manifestation of St. Padre Pio, my muse, my creative unconscious, my transcendent self, Divine Spirit, the Logos, or just you, I don't know; but whatever you are, you have given me solace and comfort whenever I turned to you; so, thank you Padre."

"You're welcome, my friend…"

———

About the Author

Born with a spiritual restlessness that could not be tamed by my Christian faith, I became a spiritual seeker when I discovered reincarnation in Plato's Dialogues at the age of fifteen. I grew up in a small town in Northwestern Ontario, and at twenty-one I had my own pool hall and vending machine business, but my restless spirit called me away to seek out my destiny, and I sold my business and sailed to France.

In the Alpine city of Annecy, in the Haute-Savoie region of France I had a dream that called me to my destiny. I entered into the mind of every person in the world and took every question they had ever asked and reduced them all to one question: *Why am I?* I returned to Canada and went to university to study philosophy to seek an answer to this haunting question, and by "chance" I discovered Gurdjieff, the redoubtable teacher of a system of transformative thought that he called "the Work." His Teaching excited my restless spirit and compelled me to seek out the answer to man's disquieting question in the fast, often tumultuous currents of daily living.

Visit him at: http://ostocco.wix.com/ostocco
Spiritual Musings Blog:
http://www.spiritualmusingsbyoreststocco.blogspot.com

ALSO BY OREST STOCCO

POETRY

Not My Circus, Not My Monkeys

NOVELS

The Golden Seed
Tea with Grace
Jesus Wears Dockers
Healing with Padre Pio
Keeper of the Flame
My Unborn Child
On the Wings of Habitat
What Would I Say Today If I Were to Die Tomorrow?

NON-FICTION

My Writing Life
Death, the Final Frontier
The Merciful Law of Divine Synchronicity
Gurdjieff Was Wrong But His Teaching Works
The Man of God Walks Alone
The Summoning of Noman
The Lion that Swallowed Hemingway
The Sum of All Spiritual Paths
Do We Have An Immortal Soul?
Stupidity Is Not a Gift of God
Letters to Padre Pio
Old Whore Life
Just Going with the Flow
Why Bother? The Riddle of the Good Samaritan
The Pearl of Great Price
In The Shade of the Maple Tree

www.ingramcontent.com/pod-product-compliance
Lightning Source LLC
Chambersburg PA
CBHW021052090426
42738CB00006B/302